Archie Sparrow's Book of Useful Tips to Beat the Recession with Baling String

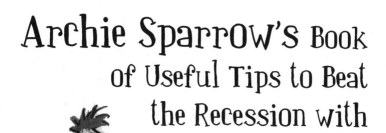

'The Tight B*st*rd's Guide to Running a Smallholding'

by
Dave Dealy

With cartoons by the talented
Mr Ken Wignall,
another Lancashire lad

Published by The Good Life Press Ltd. 2010
(but only once they signed my non-disclosure agreement - I
didn't want them blagging to all their lah-de-dah publishing
luvvies about my ideas!)

ISBN 978 1 90487 1767

A catalogue record for this book is available from
the British Library

Published by
The Good Life Press Ltd.
The Old Pigsties
Clifton Fields
Lytham Road
Preston
PR4 0XG

www.goodlifepress.co.uk
www.homefarmer.co.uk

Printed in the UK by CPI Anthony Rowe
(but alas not in Lancashire)

Note from publisher
to editor

This guy is either
fantastic or a nutter!
Has this got wings?

Note from editor
to publisher

Don't touch it
with a barge
pole!!!!!

ARCHIE SPARROW'S BIOGRAPHY

Archie is a middle-aged northern smallholder who lives with his long suffering wife Jenny. Archie's father was an ex-Coronation mug engraver and river Irwell deck chair attendant. He met Archie's mother at Appleby Horse Fair and they got married at the Pendle Co-op store. Their honeymoon was spent walking round Preston flea market looking for tartan paint, sky hooks, a long stand and a bucket of steam! They moved (Jenny pushed the wheel barrow) into Jenny's ancestral farm known as 'Not Painted Green Gables.' Archie was conceived in 1947 but born in 1953. His parents were that poor that the woman on the next farm gave birth to him. Archie's father bought her a fur coat (a donkey jacket!) in return for her 'labour.' Archie married his childhood sweetheart and "loose bike chain fixer" Jenny in 1981. It was similar to Charles' and Diana's wedding, except Jenny made her own dress using a gas mask and some net curtains and Archie insisted that HP sauce be placed on the 'top table.'

They have never been blessed with children and are still in possession of a full book of Green Shield stamps.

A Border Collie, Heinz 57, (sometimes called Lassie and sometimes Molly), resides with Jenny and Archie. They once had a Border Collie cat but it left home due to lack of food. Archie asked, "What's it need food for? There are plenty of house mice to catch."

He is a cross between Alf Garnett and Andy Capp (minus all their redeeming features), but with a tractor (a Ford 3000), a donkey jacket, Wellington boots and a flat cap.

He spends most of his days warming his backside on the fire as he shouts profanities at the television. He particularly dislikes newsreaders and Alan Titchmarsh.

Archie acquired the bulk of his worldly wisdom at 'the school of real life' and honed it by putting the world to rights in his local pub, The Dog & Goldfish.

Archie's hobbies include cows, pigs, hens, ducks, supping ale, collecting baling string (of course!), putting the world to rights, growing vegetables, supping yet more ale and putting the world to rights (again). If he had his way we'd have no need of this coalition stuff and nonsense!

ACKNOWLEDGMENTS

There are many people and animals to thank for the writing of Archie Sparrow. You all know who you are and I thank you with all my heart. You have helped fulfil my longstanding dream to be a published writer. And many thanks to my publishers at The Good Life Press Ltd. too!

Dave Dealy
November 2010

INTRODUCTION

I am a poor old farmer and I grow weary listening to politicians, taxi drivers, licensed victuallers and the missus rattling on about the Credit Crunch. It is nothing new to me, you know. I have decided that it is time I shared some of my frugal and penny pinching tips to help the likes of the Chancellor of the ex-checkers. I will show them how to save a few bob.

Your Humble Serpent,

Archie sparrow

CONTENTS

Did I tell you about my tip for using baling string for tying up fence posts?

1. BALING STRING FOR TYING UP FENCE POSTS

Old McDonald (no relation!) is known to have the finest herd of Friesian cows this side of New Zealand. They're really fine fellows and they complement his tractor. She's almost brand new and he treats her better than he treats his wife. If the truth be known he's spent more on his tractors in the last ten or twenty years than he's spent on the missus. Well, that's not strictly true. He did take her to get an 'O' ring for his muck spreader about two months ago and they stopped for a sandwich on the way home at the petrol station.

Now McDonald, he is careful with his money. He does not believe in paying for new fence posts or chains and locks for his fields. He uses baling string for all operations related to closing and exiting his fields. One morning I saw him come over the hill and stop outside the meadow gate next to my field. I was stood sheltering under an old hawthorn hedge while her 'who must who must be obeyed' was cleaning out the cattle. I saw McDonald climb down from his mighty beast of a tractor. She sounds like a dragon that's swallowed a turbo. Mind you so does his wife, but that's another story.

He then spends five minutes untying and untangling all the knots in the baling string holding up a broken gatepost. He resembled a drowned rat as he stood there in the deluge. I could hear him cursing and swearing like a priest on his (or her - mustn't be sexist!) holidays. Finally he climbs back into the tractor and tears round the field spreading his cow slurry. McDonald does grow the finest docks and nettles in Lancashire.

Archie's Top Tip

To reduce the likelihood of over exertion or even injury whilst cleaning out the cattle, get your wife to do it!

I bet he wasn't in the flipping field ten minutes emptying that slurry tank. He turned his poor fields into gutters. He then stopped his tractor with the engine still running and Terry Wogan blaring from the radio, putting the world to rights in the little meadow. McDonald then climbs out of the tractor, closes the gate and stands up the old broken and world weary fence post. He then proceeds to put on a NEW piece of baling string.

This took him five more minutes of suffering and endurance from the unrelenting rain. Well worth suffering for it was, though: after all, a new fence post would have cost at least two pounds to replace.

I need a belt to hold up my breeches. The wife is starving me to death. I'll have to be careful walking home from the pub. I might fall down the cracks in the pavement. The council never fix them proper. I wouldn't pay them with brass washers. I'm always slipping in that dog *excitement (Editor's note does he mean excrement?). Here's a tip for using baling string to hold up your kecks (trousers).

2. BALING STRING FOR HOLDING UP YOUR TROUSERS

Baling string is an ideal resource for holding up trousers. It is cheap, natural and makes a bespoke fit for that fashionable 'man about the meadow' look. Knowledge of knots is a definite advantage, though. I recommend the sheet bend knot for holding up the breeches, but please remember that trousers are not like their long-john cousins that you see in cowboy films with an escape patch in the back.

So why is a farmer so good at his job? Because he is always out standing in his field, of course!

And did you hear about the magic farm tractor? It went up the road and turned into a field.

ATTENTION! Would all farmers please contact your farm advisor immediately to see if baling string is part of your plan for next year. Be sure to tell them that you are using baling string on your trousers to fence off all your watercourses. This may affect your Single Farm Payment.

I have had to use some of my beer tokens to send a parcel to the wife's mother. It's her birthday. I have sent her some donkey stones to clean her front step. The postage will break me. Here's a tip for using baling string for tying up your parcels.

3. BALING STRING FOR TYING UP YOUR PARCELS

Baling string is excellent for tying up parcels (and their recipients or senders, in some cases). Do you remember Aunt Gertrude or any number of obscure relatives sending you an 'excellent' book on Egyptian archaeology for your 18th birthday? Twenty cigarettes, a crate of Guinness or the keys to a new car would certainly have been far more useful from the tight old bint.

Tying up your dear old aunt up with baling string would be very worthwhile and could also be very therapeutic for you. She could be transformed into a most excellent and efficient draught excluder using baling string and some old plastic silage wrappings. It would also save you having to pay to get rid of the stuff.

When you use baling string to wrap up your presents tell all your organic conscious relations that baling string is like 'real, organic nylon.' Tell them that you bought it from some hippy fellow at your local farmers' market and he said it is a 'handmade textile that's been hand woven, is carbon neutral, footprint-free and it carries with it no air miles!

It's now haymaking time on our little farm in Lancashire and we are making small hay bales this year, but my throat feels like the bottom of a birdcage. I'm spitting feathers for a brew. "Take your time, Jenny. Don't carry more than three at a time." Here's one of my baling string tips for making hay bales.

4. BALING STRING FOR HAY BALES

Long ago everything was black and white, especially that photograph of you stark naked when you were two which your old queen (mother) always insisted on showing to your prospective girlfriends. The girl would always turn and say, "He's not much bigger than that now!" In those days people, in particular farmers who needed it for their job, would attempt to make hay for their cows for the winter. Haymaking was once as important to a farmer as the correct method of making a cup of tea.

Loose hay became a thing of the past and loose women became the preferred choice of distraction. At this time the baling machine came into play. Barn dances used the bales as improvised furniture and the two pronged pitchfork got a day off. Horses and carts were suddenly made redundant and friendly neighbours who in the past had helped with the harvest were now told "Have ye no homes to go to." My pub landlord always used to say "If I don't see you in the week, I'll see you through the window." If anyone can tell me what he meant I'll be dead grateful.

Archie's Top Tip

Not a lot of people know this: baling string is great for tying up hay bales!

The hay and straw bale did revolutionize farming. The hay baler actually resembled an incontinent chicken laying its winter fodder eggs all over the field, but at least you now had something to sit on and wonder at the marvels of the devil's own machine that could wrap a piece of string on four sides, knot it and give it a neat trim.

The hay baler would then leave you to do the really hard work as you lifted, heaved, pushed and stacked it all onto a trailer. This then all had to be unloaded again and stacked in a barn in a neat and cuboid-like fashion.

Next morning you would walk around bent double like the hunchback of Notre Dame on a haymaking holiday, not forgetting too your lovely calloused hands full of blisters on top of blisters, all caused by the baling string. I have come to the conclusion that baling string is ideal for making hay and straw bales.

The powers that be are always saying that farmers should diversify and have a finger in more than one pie. That's always been my motto.

5. USING BALING STRING TO SECURE AN EXTRA FEW DAYS ACCOMMODATION FROM YOUR B&B CUSTOMERS

We all know how things are at present. There is never a day when we don't hear about the CREDIT CRUNCH and the end of the world is just a week on Friday. We are being told all the time to tighten our belts. If they care to look at tip number 2 they will see that we are already doing this.

Let me tell you a story about old Mary Lancaster, a poor spinster that lived high up on the hills overlooking Morecambe Bay. She decided to put up a BED & BREAKFAST sign in order to attract the three or four score tourists who explore these parts in summer.

She didn't used to get up until about noon, so she changed her sign to BED & SUPPER. Well bacon is rather expensive and she didn't want any foreign fly-by-nights not born in her virginity* hanging about in her kitchen when she was nursing a hangover.

* (Ed: vicinity?)

Mary Lancaster welcomed a young man and woman into her humble commode, I mean abode. The couple came from over the water. They lived on the other side of a bridge in the Lake District. I think the man used to be a banana straightener or something similar and she used to work in a jeweller's forking out all the muck from their cuckoo clocks.

The couple commented on the beautiful scenery and asked about places of interest to visit. Miss Lancaster said that they should make sure to visit the broken biscuit factory in Dolphinholme. She said the factory had had only two visitors last year. "Crumbs," said the tourists, but Mary assured them they gave you more than just crumbs.

The young couple enjoyed their stay at 'Slatted House View.' Well, at least they did until they told Mary that they only wanted to stay for the one night. Mary Lancaster had other ideas. She waited until the couple had gone to bed and she went out to the barn, collected some baling string and tied up the couple's door. This effectively ensured that the couple involuntarily agreed to pay for another night's accommodation. Baling string is very useful if you wish to run a successful BED & BREAKFAST (or SUPPER) establishment, but it doesn't guarantee you get all your stars if you pick on the wrong guests. But you can't have everything in life.

My father and mother were reluctant to have electricity installed on the farm. The only bill they ever had belonged to one of the ducks! People just don't know how to play 'monsters in the dark' anymore. It must have been great going to bed long ago when you had just eaten your tea. Here's one of my more cultural tips for using baling string to give yourself a reading light.

6. USING BALING STRING TO GIVE YOURSELF A LIGHT

Patrick Metcalfe is a confirmed bachelor farmer. He does not believe in creature comforts like electricity, water or television. If he wants a wash he uses the waterfall behind the cow stall. If he wants to watch the big match on the old goggle box invented by that Scottish Fellow Yogi Bear he saunters down to the Dog and Goldfish where he meets the lads, drinks some pints and washes it all down with a 'tater pie. What more could a man want?

Eventually, after putting the world to rights and singing 'Goodnight Irene' for the three hundredth time, he gets home and falls through the door and over the sacks of bagged manure (an awfully costly fertilizer), the dog and all manner of flotsam and jetsam like the turning handle of a Bulldog Laing tractor that a threshing contractor left behind in 1948.

Old farmer Metcalfe took out his baling string and strapped his flash lamp to the old iron bedstead. He takes off his boots and decides to read his unfinished book, 'Memoirs of a

ARCHIE SPARROW'S BOOK OF USEFUL TIPS.....

Cart Horse and Part-time Animal Detective by G.G. Dunnit. Baling string makes a cheap and state of the art light fitting and reading aid and is therefore part of the nation's cultural heritage, at least in the more rural areas.

My back tooth isn't half starting
to give me gip, but I'm not paying
to go and see yon dentist. I will
use some of my baling string to
cure it. Read on and I will save
you a few more bob!

7. BALING STRING FOR PULLING A TOOTH

Extracting a tooth can be very expensive and not everybody can afford to be a member of BUPA, the RSPCA or was it VHS? Personally I preferred Betamax to watch my videos, but it never seemed to catch on.

So what do you do if you can't afford to go to see a dentist in some posh town or Bulgaria? (Let's not forget that not everybody wants cheap food and a pint of lager for a Euro or whatever currency they use there!) I would much rather stay at home and count the stones in my dry stone walls. They are really interesting with their 'bucks and does' and 'througher' stones.

Take a piece of baling string about ten feet long and attempt to tie it to the offending tooth that has been giving you the old gip. A mirror might be a useful additional aid here. If you have children wait until it is time for them to go to bed, then attach the string to the door in the room where you relax. Now speak in a clear and coherent voice and say, "Please turn off your television now, dear child, it is time for bed." At the same time brace yourself and fasten your imaginary seatbelt.

19

Your beloved child will suddenly develop the temper of a Leprechaun with a poteen induced hangover and will most likely slam the door with all the force of a tornado and your troublesome tooth will fly out and trouble you no more (so long as the door shuts in the correct direction, otherwise you will look very stupid with a piece of loose baling string attached to your painful tooth with no immediate hope of salvation!)

Yes you will suffer a slight sensation of pain, and your room may need redecorating to remove the bloodstains, but at least you will have had your tooth removed in the comfort of your own home and you will have found yet another cost saving use for your discarded baling string.

The wife's been reading the magazines in the doctor's waiting room again. I hope she doesn't find my copies of 'Big Girls weekly' she now wants some new soft furnishings. I will never have any money while I remain married to Jenny. Here's one of my more stylish baling string tips for hanging your curtains.

8. BALING STRING FOR HANGING YOUR CURTAINS UP

John Matthews and his new wife Rosie moved into their house on their wedding day. It was that cold a house that even the rats wore fur coats. Dear old Rosie was of a cheerful disposition though. She came from a musical family as her mother had owned a Singer sewing machine.

A condition of Rosie marrying John was that he allowed her to put curtains up in the bedroom window. Although John could see no possible reason for this ludicrous extravagance, he did concede defeat in ruling that part of the bedroom. The house was well over a hundred years old and there was certainly no evidence of an earlier curtain rail as nobody had ever seen the need for it either. John had always thought to himself that if people wanted to walk past their front window and see them in their birthday suits, that was entirely up to them.

Rosie would have none of it, though. She was showing her body to nobody but her intended and even that was only to be done infrequently. She got out her sewing machine and

21

ran up two curtains made out of two flour sacks. She may have had middle class notions about soft furnishings but she clearly shared John's thrift!

She was delighted with her work and showed her new curtains to her husband. Her next problem was the lack of a curtain rail or any string to hold them up. Necessity is the mother of invention and a toilet if ever you're dying for a wee, so John went out to his shed and returned (like the hunter, gatherer he most certainly was) with a length of old baling string, a hammer and two horse shoe nails.

He set to work and attempted to bang the nails into the old lime plaster. The walls had more cracks in them than a hen's egg after breakfast. John cursed and huffed and wheezed and swore again. He hit one nail that hard that it ricocheted off a wall, onto another and landed in the chamber pot under their bed. He searched everywhere for it but he could not find it. Eventually, in desperation, Rosie suggested emptying the overflowing chamber pot but John, true to form, said, "I only do it twice a year."

Rosie picked up the offensive item and marched off down the stairs. She came back a few minutes later and said, "Look what I've found." He looked down at the now empty chamber pot. There in the bottom of the container was the nail that had gone astray. John picked it up and placed it carefully in his mouth as builders short of another pair of hands are wont to do. He then said, somewhat optimistically, "Thanks. I don't suppose you found my false teeth in there as well?"

Eventually they assembled the curtains using the baling string and Rosie made a point of never kissing John ever again.

our Lassie is as daft as a box of frogs lately. she wants me to take her for a walk past the vicarage. I think it's the vicar's new Border collie she's interested in. It's a male and it barks right posh, so here's one of my baling string tips for a dog lead.

9. BALING STRING FOR TAKING ONE'S DOGGIE FOR A WALK

There is something to be said for taking a walk with a dog, unless of course it is the dog that takes you for the walk. One absolutely vital piece of equipment for dog walking is a leash or a lead. (I once had a dog who wanted to take the lead and star in Lassie) and leads come in all colours, shapes and materials; they can be made of leather, chain or textile.

I personally recommend or prefer the Hippy, Eco-Warrior method. I am not talking about a new organic kind of contraception, (although baling string, a gluten free bread bag and some more baling string might well do the job! Yet another use for baling string!). I am talking about using baling string to take one's tripe hound for a saunter.

Ask yourself how many times you turn your house upside down looking for the dog lead? Can you find it? Can you flip. There is more chance of dialling random numbers on your phone and getting Johnny Logan singing "What's Another Year?" or the Queen asking if you are you coming round for a brew?

Archie's Top Tip

A friend in need is a
bloody nuisance!

As you rummage about through your chest of drawers you will always find an endless supply of indispensable items; half eaten Mars bars, broken corkscrews, an old lawnmower manual for a machine that committed Hari Kiri twenty years ago, some rusty nails, a hub cap, a few Greek Drachmas and that flat cap that used to belong to the man who delivered milk to Churchill's fifth cousin. But can you ever find the dog lead? There is more chance of finding the meaning of life in that chest of drawers. But worst of all, why did you ask Rover if he wanted to go walkies before you started looking for the lead?

Fear not, dog walker and wife escaper. Brush yourself down, wash your face and remove those doggy kisses and canine hugs.

Have you recovered now? Good! So find yourself a piece of baling string and attach it to your dog. You can now relax and go for a stroll with your furry friend. Remember, always keep some baling string in your pocket for dog walking or in that chest of drawers for whatever life throws at you.

I recently ran over a stone in the
gorse field I think it might have been
a remnant from that Glacier family
who own Manchester United. Anyway, it
broke one of my tractor's mudguards.
short of being able to sue the Glaciers
it's a good job that I had some baling
string. Here is a tip for using baling
string to fix your tractor.

10. BALING STRING FOR HOLDING YOUR TRACTOR TOGETHER

Baling string is exceptionally strong and is ideal for holding your tractor parts together. Muck spreaders and manure spreaders simply thrive on them. If the truth be known, rural Britain has been held together by the stuff for decades. Why pay for expensive nuts, bolts, brackets and screws?

Baling string also comes in many different colours. Blue is ideally suited for the Ford and New Holland models. I recommend red baling string for Massey Fergusons, green for John Deere of course, orange for Kubotas and Zetors, whilst white is apt for the David Browns. The list is colossal and baling string manufacturers should take note of this fact. Please expand your coloured baling string catalogue as necessary.

Perhaps when purchasing your next tractor it might be advisable to take a piece of baling string along with you? Don't be misled by the black arts of eager sales representatives as they attempt to confuse you with irrelevancies such as horse power, torque satnav and tinted sunroofs or even their offer of plastic mud should you need to go on a protest in the city. No, the burning question on the tip of every prospective farmer's tongue should be, "Will the paintwork match my baling string?"

Have you ever met a bus or train spotter? They hang around bus and train stations, particularly on sunday mornings, writing down the numbers of the trains or buses and comparing notes and peanut sandwiches with other cagoule clad spotters. Here's a more rewarding hobby...

11. WHY NOT BE A BALING STRING COLLECTOR?

Here in rural Britain I see a new hobby, nay craze, about to sweep the nation. Am I talking about vintage tractors, Morris dancing (whoever he is?) or the Badminton horse trials? No! I can think of a far more interesting and rewarding pastime and soon to become for some an obsession. Become a baling string collector. It is guaranteed non-addictive to most normal people and will prevent the problem of marrying the wrong person (or any person, for that matter).

"Whatever happened to Val Doonican?" I hear you all asking? I wonder if he wants to sell any of his old cardigans. He used to sing a song called Paddy McGinty's Goat. It unfortunately swallowed some dynamite. Here's one of my baling string tips for tethering a goat.

12. BALING STRING FOR TETHERING A GOAT

If you ever have the desire to get yourself a goat you will find a tether is a must. Goats are the spawn of the devil. They don't have twin towns, instead they have suicide pacts. A goat will eat you out of house, home and every garden shrub. They are browse grazers. Give them the finest grass and they will turn their nose up and say, "Thanks very much, but I would prefer a shirt or a pair of trousers off your washing line."

If you buy or are unlucky enough to be given a goat, make sure that you tether it. Ten pieces of baling string plaited together might just hold a nanny goat. A puck goat or a Billy goat will need nothing less than a ship's anchor and steel cables to moor the creature. They have the strength of an ox and stink to high heaven of urine too. Or was that Mrs Littlewood who used to deliver the post,

All in all, baling string is an excellent low-tech restraining apparatus for a goat.

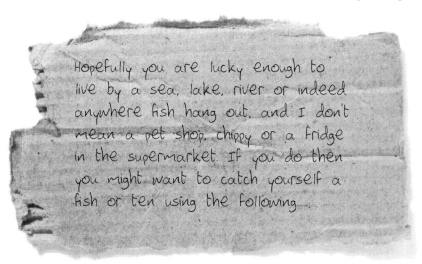

Hopefully you are lucky enough to
live by a sea, lake, river or indeed
anywhere fish hang out, and I don't
mean a pet shop, chippy or a fridge
in the supermarket. If you do then
you might want to catch yourself a
fish or ten using the following.....

13. BALING STRING FOR FISHING NETS

You can do this by getting some baling string and sewing
yourself a net. It will give you more hours of pleasure than
any jigsaw and you might even make yourself a few bob.

There are all manner of nets to make like fishing nets or purse
nets for catching rabbits. Then there is Annette too, which is
a woman's name. You will have made yourself a lady friend
in the process, but don't use the net to catch her or you will
get yourself arrested. Now take the net to sea and see what
you will catch. If you catch crabs, blame Annette.

Are the wife and pigeons alright? Here's one of my baling string tips for storing onions that you've grown on your allotment. I hope you haven't been growing any of them funny marrow-banana (marijuana) plants. Remember hemp is never as strong as baling string!

14. BALING STRING FOR STRINGING ONIONS.

Have you ever been to France and seen those beret wearing Frenchmen riding around on bicycles with crusty long bread sticks and strings of onions? No, I haven't either. It's a bit like the Loch Ness monster and politicians telling the truth. They are all works of fiction.

Although I did read that Elvis Presley owns a video rental shop near Kendal. Or was it a haberdashery store?

If you grow alliums (their Sunday name) then you might wish to learn how to string them up. Baling string could certainly be used for this purpose and it is a cheap and rewarding hobby. The only other thing that you will need is onions.

Here's another of my baling string tips: if you are about to have a night on the tiles (No I don't mean sleeping on the roof) then here's a baling string tip for a sleeping line.

15. BALING STRING FOR A SLEEPING LINE

If you plan on having a few drinks with your mates I recommend that you take a length of baling string with you. The string needs to be long enough to tie to both a tree and to your drainpipe.

Let us imagine we are a fly on the wall of your local hostelry. It is getting near to 'throwing out time' and you suddenly notice that the pub has had revolving walls installed. You quite rightly think it appropriate that you should tell your drinking acquaintance that he is the bestest, zestiest, testiest friend in the world. Also you notice that the old spinster supping the milk stout has suddenly been transformed from a bulldog chewing a wasp into the potential next Miss World. The landlord kindly but forcefully helps you through the door of his establishment. You then place one foot on the pavement and one foot on the road. It is now time to walk in a straight line to prove to everybody that you are in no way drunk.

You then decide that you will go to the local Chinese takeaway and order 'everything.' You have never entered into one of these establishments before or ever tasted their cuisine and there is only one thing to do in such a situation: You find yourself saying, "I will have ten pounds worth please." The takeaway counter person says, "Ten pounds of what?" You in turn reply, "Of everything."

You and your drinking friend then stagger home. It is now you discover that you do not like Oriental food and decide to post some through the Employment Office letterbox for all the 'lovely people' to enjoy first thing on Monday morning.

Eventually at about half past four you stagger down the road. "Look," says your drinking buddy, "It's your wife." There before your eyes you can just make out the missus stood there with a face like thunder and the frying pan in one hand. "Yes," you slur and fall over onto that beloved hydrangea her mother once gave her for her wedding anniversary.

"What a wife you've got," says your friend. "Imagine cooking breakfast for us at this time of night."

You bid farewell to your drinking friend and the wife slams the front door in your face. Now is the time to search in your pocket and remove that now furry sticky toffee covered in hairs and the length of baling string I mentioned earlier. Tie one end to the drain-pipe and the other end to a tree. Now place one arm on the line and lean on it. I bid you goodnight.

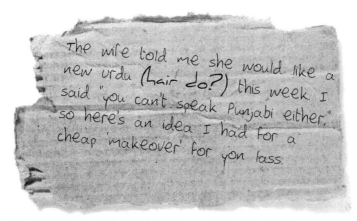

The wife told me she would like a new urdu (hair do?) this week. I said "you can't speak Punjabi either," so here's an idea I had for a cheap 'makeover' for yon lass.

16. BALING STRING FOR HAIR BRAIDS.

There is one film always worth a gander. It's called '10' and stars Bo Derek. She's beautiful and fit as a butcher's dog (never understood that saying: a butchers dog should be fat). She would make the sap rise in the trees when it's winter.

Buy it for you and the wife to watch late at night. You might also have to buy her a sack of Mars bars and her favourite cocktail, a Bulmer's cider and Toby light.

Before you treat this special lady, the love of your life, this flower of the Orient and wicked witch of the west, please pay particular attention to the following piece of advice: if your wife is reaching the autumn of her life and her mane is not quite what it once was, then pop into the builder's merchant and get yourself a tub of the strongest plumber's glue you can find.

When you have watched the film and she is starting to get in the mood, or better still asleep, take out twenty four one foot (30cm if you've been metricized) lengths of baling string and attach them to the wife's head with the plumbers glue and make your wife's hair into a white Rastafarian style. Hey presto, you now have your own little Bo Derek. Wake her up and tell her to look in the mirror. I am sure she will give you a surprise.

There's nowt on the telly at the moment (since I knocked off one of the wife's ornaments when I came home after a night at the Dog and Goldfish). The telly's not working any more either so we are thinking of taking up a hobby. Here's a baling string tip for macramé.

17. BALING STRING FOR MACRAMÉ

You know those long winter evenings when you are mentally doing your non-academic studies in boredom? The wife is telling you to shut up while she watches the inhabitants of Weatherfield engaging in gossip and drinking copious amounts of Newton and Ridley bitter. You are sat thinking, 'Why can't they put on a blue movie or a farming programme about Harry Ferguson and his three point linkage.'

It's precisely at times like this when a country farmer needs a hobby, so why not learn about the ancient craft of macramé. No, it is not an Island near Pavarotti. It is something that you do with your hands on your own. I know what you're thinking, and NO, it will not make you go blind or if it does it won't be for that reason!

Macramé is quite a cheap hobby and your ever reliable baling string can be used in your new pastime and it will reduce the cost even further if you are prepared to use whatever colour you have lying around the shed.

Macramé is the skill and art of knotting string or cord into geometric patterns and is thus very similar to a devious EEC farming policy maker. Sailors have used it to make knots of squares and triangular forms to decorate anything from a butter knife to a friendship bracelet.

Archie's Top Tip

Rome wasn't built in a day. Perhaps that's because they had no baling string!

That's it! I have the perfect solution to your problem with your neighbour who owns the holiday home on Fitton's Farm. Yes, I know you have had your run ins with the family and I know he doesn't like your cows staring over the hedge when they are having their supper. And didn't he once ask you if you would only spread your slurry when they are not here? Yes, I know he refused to put a gate on his entrance and plays merry hell if your cows decide to have a nibble on his lovely lush landscaped lawns.

They say tourism is the future for the small farmer, so next time your neighbour tries to show you that he rules the roost, simply rush out with your home-made baling string 'friendship bracelet' and greet him like a long lost friend. It may not serve to help you both put earlier misunderstandings behind you but it will be guaranteed to both worry and confuse him with regard to any future encounters between the two of you and that will be more than ample compensation for all the efforts you have made.

I personally hate neighbours. 'Home and Away' isn't much better either for that matter and you never ever see that skippy the Bush Kangaroo any more. To compensate here's one of my tips for dealing with neighbours who won't shut their gates.

18. BALING STRING FOR TYING UP YOUR NEIGHBOURS' GATES.

Right! You have tried to be friendly to the people who have the holiday home, but it is all to no avail. Your friendship bracelet has been returned and they still will not shut their gate, so you have to spend ten minutes going and shutting their gate for them before you can move your cattle along the leafy track to their pasture for the day. There is now only one thing to do and yes, it does involve some baling string.

Wait until it is absolutely throwing it down and the puddles resemble lakes. As soon as your neighbours go out for their copy of either 'Anti-Social Weekly' or 'Fascism for Holiday Breaks,' tie up their gate with the baling string. Make at least twenty of your finest knots and then retire to wait in anticipation for your 'friendly holiday home neighbour' to return from their shopping adventures. They are sure not to have brought any scissors with them and will take on the appearance of drowned rats as they struggle to overcome your finest attempts to maintain bio-security on the farm. At least you know you have been a good neighbour and shut their gate for them! It's what the country code is all about.

The wife now wants an electric fire for christmas. I ~~would~~ rather buy her an electric chair. But here's a baling string tip for lighting your fire to keep you warm.

19. BALING STRING FOR LIGHTING THE FIRE

Have you seen the price of fire lighters these days? I won't pay those extravagant prices just to light my fire. I find myself in the same frame of mind as Mrs Bradley who was buying toilet paper in the Co-op store just the other week. Mrs Bradley says, "How much are your toilet rolls, Mrs Cunningham?" She replies, "Three pounds." Mrs Bradley shook her head and said, "I am not paying that for what I want them for."

In these days of credit crunching we have to find ways of saving our pennies, or rather pence. Baling string is excellent for lighting fires along with unopened bills and charity leaflets. I personally treat all charities the same and always give them equal amounts, and that's precisely nothing!

Archie's Top Tip

Too many cooks make too many dinners.

37

ARCHIE SPARROW'S BOOK OF USEFUL TIPS.....

Use baling string to light the fire but remember not to light it until at least four in the afternoon. Better still, look out your door and check if there is any smoke coming out of anybody's chimney. If they're poachers they will give themselves away by not having their fire reddened. If you spot any smoke coming out of a chimney, call round on your neighbour and get a free warming; they might even give you a drink or ten?

Yes I know they will bring out all those boring holiday photographs and show you the picture of that nice couple the Burtons who sat at table two in that bed and breakfast in Blackpool. But they do always keep a large bottle of whiskey ready for your visit. Isn't it better to be plastered with a bore than sober with a saint?

If they should then call round on you after you invited them to call round out of a drunken but misplaced politeness after drinking all their whiskey, be sure to use baling string and an old sock to gag the wife and pretend you're not in! Jump down behind the couch if necessary and tell her it's the rent collector.

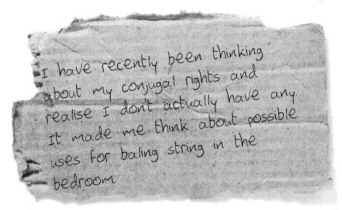

I have recently been thinking about my conjugal rights and realise I don't actually have any. It made me think about possible uses for baling string in the bedroom

20. BALING STRING TO TIE UP THE MISSUS.

Is your sex life becoming a bit repetitive and rather dull, or even non-existent? The missionary position is possibly the only position your wife will let you practice on your birthday as she coos sweet nothings about the ceiling needing a coat of paint or asking you to remove the cobwebs from the lightshade? At this point there is only one thing for you to do; get out your baling string and tie up the old girl. Tell her you fancy getting kinky and wouldn't mind trying a game of bondage (or should that be bailage?).

Be sure not to get yourself in the same predicament as poor old Michael Davenport. He told his friend that he was going through the forty seven year itch and he wanted something that would add a bit of spice to his marital bed. His friend Patrick suggested that he should try a bit of the old S & M, to which Michael said he didn't want to go shopping in a well known English department store. Pat realized he had got his wires crossed and said, "Not M & S, I mean S & M. That Sadie Massacre schism kind of thing." Davenport said he had never heard of the woman, but he wouldn't mind having ago at tying up the missus!

So that night after drinking lots of Dutch courage (Whiskey and a Thwaites bitter), Michael Davenport said to his wife over supper, "Pass me the salt and would you like to be tied up with no clothes on?" Mrs Davenport didn't even bat an eyelid. "I will if you let me tie you up first, Mick."

Michael wolfed down his bacon and cabbage and ran outside for some baling string. He then went upstairs, threw off his clothes and said, "Tie me to the old iron bedstead please, my dear." Ever the faithful and doting wife Mrs Davenport tied the naked Michael to the bed, shut the bedroom and ran down the stairs to watch Eastenders.

A couple of hours later the phone rang. It was Mick's friend Pat. Mrs Davenport said, "I am afraid Michael can't come to the phone at the moment, he's tied up for the evening."

Isn't meat dear (Ed: deer?) now or is it just venison? Here's one of my favourite baling string tips for catching rabbits.

21. BALING STRING FOR CATCHING RABBITS.

I think the Credit Crunch is really biting. Are you short of a few bob for a few slurps or ten to escape from 'her who must be obeyed?' Why not have a go at catching those fellows with the big ears and the twitching noses? No, I don't mean those politicians who come canvassing for your vote. I am talking about the lads who get up at the crack of dawn to eat your precious grass, the rabbits. They infuriate you and make you curse and swear, but they can also be quite a problem.

When you where young rabbit pie was a staple diet item and, like pig muck, it wasn't something to be sniffed at. Old Harry Ferguson (God rest his tractor) used to have a novel way of catching rabbits. He would find a nest of young rabbits and give them to the neighbouring children to look after and nurture. The kids would take them home and fatten them with the best food bought from the Co-op. Then, six months later, Harry would call and replace the fat bunnies with more baby ones and Harry would walk away with his supper.

We can't all be that resourceful, so why not use baling string to make a snare. One of those lasso like thingumajigs that you peg near to one of your lettuces will do, but be careful what you catch and be quiet when you decide to put your victim out of his or her misery.

I know a fellow who once set a snare to catch a giant rabbit that kept pinching his vegetables. He only ended up snaring the vicar. The vicar said that he was, "merely looking at the wonders of God's bountiful and wondrous creation." My friend nodded his head and said, "Yes, I agree. Look, there's a bunch of carrots growing out of your pocket!"

At my time of life I think it's time I took life at a more leisurely pace. Margaret Thatcher and winston Churchill both had a lie down in the afternoon, but I don't think they did it together. If it's good enough for them, it's good enough for Archie sparrow, so here's a baling string tip for making a hammock.

22. BALING STRING FOR A HAMMOCK.

If we ever get a summer you can easily make yourself a hammock out of baling string. I hope it's better than last year which only lasted a day. Still you can always do some rain bathing in your long johns. Rain is God's way of giving you a free wash. Anyway, you know those things that they tie between two trees or two cow's tails? You can curl up and have a Ford Fiesta (Siesta-Lancashire rhyming slang) in. They're great for lying in and supervising the missus as she mows the lawn. Is yours anything like my darling wife? Good at pushing the mower, but rubbish at getting the stripes symmetrical. She said we should buy a petrol one with GPS or a satnav. I said you can't buy a hammock that runs on petrol. She suddenly transformed into a banshee and shouted, "A petrol mower, you pudding!" I don't know, you train them to operate a pedestrian powered mower and they want to be the boss.

The wife's stormed off now and left me with half a mowed lawn. It looks like I've been sprinkling whiskey on it. It's come up half cut! Now I need a lie down on my hammock. The wife's just given me a serious hook with the frying pan.

43

The crows have been at my cabbages again. I don't know how they get into the flipping supermarket. You don't think I grow them, do you? I was watching that John Peartree in wurzel Gummidge last night and I told Jenny she looks like that Aunt Sally. She punched me in the gob and now I'm like wurzel I've got my 'sulking head' on. Here's a baling string tip to make a scarecrow. My talent is seriously wasted Jenny says I should work for NASA and become Lancashire's first astronaut. There's a whole universe out there hungry for the benefits of baling string.

23. BALING STRING TO MAKE A SCARECROW

Do the birds eat your vegetables? Why not make yourself a scarecrow? Get some baling string and cut yourself two blackthorn sticks and tie them into a cross. Then look in the wardrobe for some of your old clothes. What do you mean you need them all and there's plenty of wear in them yet? Do you remember when the wife asked you for a fur coat last Christmas and you bought her a donkey jacket?

Fill your spare trousers with baling string and stuff the jacket with old hay. Then make a head out of a large turnip and you will have yourself a scarecrow. Ask the wife if your scarecrow resembles Brad Pitt. "No," she will say. "He looks the spitting image of you."

we have had a lot of weather lately down on our little farm. The fields are full of rushes and dock leaves. one consolation is we don't need to buy any toilet paper. Here's one of my baling string tips to help you in the event of a disaster.

24. BALING STRING FOR TYING UP SANDBAGS

Do you remember the War? No, I am not talking about the constant battles with your mother-in-law. I am talking about the time we thought we were going to be invaded and would have to eat all that foreign muck. No longer would the meat and potato pie be the staple diet of the good and bad people of Britain. Not forgetting the ploughman's lunch, of course. I feel sorry for the ploughman. They have already replaced his horse with a tractor and now everyone is eating his lunch. They wouldn't nick a 'builder's breakfast.' Look at them in Brussels sprouts land at the EEC. Them there foreigners would make us eat brie and garlic and tomatoes and live to the ripe age of six hundred and ninety six. Or was that the number of the bus to Kendal? It didn't sell mint cake either! Bring back Selnec and Ribble buses. Imagine our poor government having to pay pensions until you're six hundred and ninety six!

You never know though. We could be invaded again and

Archie's Top Tip

Tell your kids the coin slot electricity meter is a money box!

we might have to start digging trenches and filling sandbags, this time to prepare for war and flood too as it's four years since we last had a summer. I know of a farmer called Noah who is making a wooden boat out of old bag manure (fertilizer) pallets. I asked him how he is going to hold them together. He says, "Two by two." He wants to borrow some of my baling string. I told him I'll need it to tie up my sandbags. The only problem is the price of sand. They want five hundred pounds for a lorry of sand. Then I will need to fill the bags and I will need to buy a shovel. The sandbags will need filling too. My back will be broken and I will have to get the wife to rub it.

I don't think I will bother. If the river bursts its bank and floods the farm I will let it do so and claim off the insurance for a new farm. I will wait until floods are predicted and then I'll start paying insurance every week. Ten bob a week isn't too much money to pay to get a new farm.

I will have to go now. The wife wants me to open the farm gate while she carries the ten sand bags that I have filled with the sand up to the field. Well, strictly speaking it isn't sand at all. It's what's known in farming circles as dung: cow dung to be precise. It's wet, it's heavy and it smells.

It would make a good description for the wife. She never stops complaining about having to carry out the farm tasks. It should be me who should be complaining though. She hasn't even cooked my breakfast yet!

when was the last time you had a bath? Last month? we've still got ours. But the coal we keep in it makes bathing very uncomfortable. I think my long johns could do with a few patches too and I could do with a new thermos vest. I am going to get Jenny to make me a string vest. she does more knitting than Nitty Norah, the school nit nurse. Here's a tip for using baling string to make a vest.

25. BALING STRING FOR A VEST

It's that time of year when people take their holidays. That man from the city comes for a month and stays on old Richard Arkwright's farm. He only has one set of grandparents planted in the local graveyard so he will never be 'one of the locals.' He said that his father left here in the fifties. I said he should have stopped the car first, and learn to drive at a more sensible speed.

He always brings me a bottle of whiskey as well as the wife's favourite magazine, 'The Ferret Stroker's and Rat Catcher's Weekly.' It keeps her quiet and gives her much amusement during the long, dark months.

At least he talks to me and always buys me a few glasses of Old Peculiar. He's invited us to the seaside tomorrow. It should be lovely, but I don't know what to wear. I want to look like your typical holidaymaker, in fact like the man from the city himself. I have studied his summer attire and I think that, with a little bit of thought, I will not look out of place and might just be the spitting image of him.

The wife says she will run me up a string vest out of some baling string. All I will need to do is roll up my trouser legs and find myself a knotted handkerchief to protect my ever balding head. I now look like the lad who comes 'home' for his holidays. We are going to get some deckchairs and sit on the beach and moan about the weather. It should be wonderful. I just hope the wife doesn't knit herself a bikini out of baling string.

So lads, if you want a cheap summer rig out, get yourself some baling string and make a vest.

Did you watch the olympics on the goggle box? I am going to write a letter of complaint. where were the sports that working class folk play? I am the 'shove ha'penny' champion in our local boozer. They never let you know how Britain got on at tiddlywinks either, do they? well, here's one of my baling string tips for a tug of war competition.

26. BALING STRING FOR A TUG OF WAR COMPETITION

The word is that they are trying to raise money to build a Community Centre. They should try building a community first. The wife suggested having a tug of war between our two neighbouring villages. I said that the last time there was a tug of war competition one of the sides was disqualified for pushing.

I reluctantly agreed to make a rope out of some old baling string. I spent all day plaiting twenty pieces together. It should do the job, and they will be able to count the speed they win in knots as all the pieces of the rope are knotted together!

I asked John Hargreaves, the bachelor down the road, if he was taking part, especially with the opposing team being predominantly female. I said, "It will be the only time in your life when you're able to pull a woman!"

Lancashire is world famous for its textile industry, its vimto wells and Hollands' pies. I have always had the ambition to travel to foreign parts like Chorley and Warrington New Town, but it's been a bad year for my brassicas. They are have all come down with club root and I am burdened with Lancashire trench foot. I am thinking of starting my own cottage textile industry and Jenny is making us a rug out of baling string.

27. BALING STRING FOR A RUG

Have you ever dreamed of taking off your clothes and lying stark naked with the missus on a sheepskin rug in front of the fire? No, I haven't either. The last time we had such a notion they threw us out of the lounge bar in that big hotel in Southport. We wasn't causing any trouble and it certainly didn't seem to bother the funeral party!

Anyway, the wife wants a rug. She says it would be lovely to lie in front of the fire and we could snuggle up together and have romantic moments. What do I want to act like Molly (Lassie) my sheepdog for? I would rather have piles and constipation and a blocked up septic tank than spend time chin-wagging with the missus.

The wife won't have any of it though. Ever since she started attending that well woman, haberdashery and pig farming clinic she thinks that she can do anything that takes her fancy. She even got up this morning at five o'clock and started knitting a rug made from me baling string.

I just can't cope with all these changes. Jenny will be wanting a broadband washing machine next. oh no, me mobile groan's ringing. "Yes Jenny, we'll have a brew. Put the kettle on. But I don't think it will fit you." I think it's about time we brought the farm into the 20th century. Yes, I did say 20th century, the 21st is way too advanced to think of and Buck Rogers lives there and saves the universe with his wi-fi baling string. Here's a proper hi-tech geek baling string project.

28. BALING STRING FOR MAKING AN INTERCOM

Get yourself a really long length of baling string and two tin cans. I recommend Newcastle Brown Ale. Drink them with a neighbour and moan about the price. Then get a six inch nail (or a fifteen centimetre one if you're a disciple of CAP).

Use it to make a hole in the bottom of each can with a hammer, if you can afford one. A red Accrington NORI house brick will do otherwise. Then thread your baling string through it. Place the cans at each end of the string and knot them in place. You now have a state of the art communications apparatus. The wife can call you in for supper or when it is time for bed, and you won't be able to hear a thing she says, so she won't be able to disturb you. Well, not until she belts you with the yard brush for ignoring her!

These experts on the telly keep rabbiting on about the so-called Credit Crunch. They think they know everything and they know nowt! When I was a lad we had real poverty. We didn't have the X Factor and that Fern Britton's Got Talons. We only had dolly tubs, whippet races, diphtheria and rickets.

Folk today should learn how to make do and mend things. Take our Jenny, for example. she is sewing some sleeves on a continental quilt to make a trench coat. Here is one of my own tips for mending a cushion.

29. BALING STRING FOR STUFFING A CUSHION

Is your couch like mine: all saggy and in need of stuffing? In these harsh economic times we need to make do and mend. The wife says my family have been recycling for hundreds of years. We were green before God gave the grass its colour.

I just don't believe in wasting stuff. The wife is nothing but a spendthrift. She spent ten pounds in the supermarket the other day on groceries. I would have spent nothing, except for a bottle of whiskey and some tins of bitter from the off-licence. But they're only for medicinal purposes, of course!

Archie's Top Tip

Careless talk costs wives!

Anyway, I have this couch that has cushions that need reupholstering. The lad down in the village says he wants twenty pounds to make it firm and pretty, like my wife on her wedding night. I told him I didn't' know what he was talking about, she was never pretty.

The missus wants a new couch but I will hear none of it. It was good enough for my great grandmother, so it's good enough for yours truly. I said it wouldn't need repairing if she stopped ripping it apart looking for loose change and cake crumbs. I took the bread knife and unpicked the stitches and stuffed the cushions with baling string. It feels really comfortable and I found a sixpence. I will use it if I ever need to give somebody a tip.

There was an almighty storm last night. It kept me awake all night. I even had to send the wife out to check on the cattle in the yard she informed me that they were fine, but one of the zinc sheets had detached itself from the cowshed roof and had flown down into the meadow. There's always more work to be done on a farm. Here's a baling string tip for 'feckling' the roof.

30. BALING STRING TO HOLD DOWN A CORRUGATED ROOFING SHEET

"Oh what will I do?" thinks me'self. She'll probably ladder her tights climbing up the ladder. I wouldn't mind, but I bought her a new pair last year. It's awfully expensive running a farm.

I would fix the sheet me'self, but then there would be no one to place their foot on the first rung of the ladder, a job that requires a professional touch. Somebody's got to supervise and give out the orders. Oh, and did I mention my back? I am that ill with it sometimes, even the doctor doesn't know what is wrong with me.

She said that she wants some galvanized nails to fix the roof. I said, "Do you think I am made of money?" I let go of the ladder and went and rummaged for some polypropylene baling string and Jenny made a fine job of tying the sheet in place and carrying two boulders up to hold it down. But I wish that she wouldn't wear a skirt when she climbs up the ladder. I thought I had seen an eclipse of the moon!

I don't know where her indoors gets her ideas from. she now tells me that she wants a clothes dryer. Have you ever heard such a preposterous request? I said, "The next thing you'll be wanting is running water." she was not amused and said, "Running water sounds like a red Indian." Well we've had enough cowboys doing jobs round here so we might as well have him now." If you can't do a job with baling string it isn't worth doing so here's a baling string tip for drying your clothes.

31. BALING STRING FOR DRYING YOUR CLOTHES IN THE KITCHEN

I can't be buying one of them tumble dryers. They would use far too much of the eccentricity current and we have no room for one anyway. The other half says she either gets a dryer or my dinner will be permanently in the dog.

I went to see some crusty folk who rent old farmer Smith's place. They are them hippy fellows who go to that Glastonbury festival; the sort who get out of the bath to pee in the sink. They are very sociable folk and would give you the shirts off their backs. I think they call them new age travellers, or was that a car similar to the Morris minor made of wood? I told Moon Planet (he's really called Wayne) my dilemma. He said, "Is it creating a bad Korma in your gaff?" I replied, "We don't eat curry in our house?" Then he says that we need to "chill out, guys" and we should get ourselves some "good shit." I said, "There is nothing wrong with my bowels, thank you very much! An apple a day keeps the doctor away." We then had a few gargles of his home brew and he made me a lovely magic mushroom omelette. He even sent me home with a ceiling clothes airer. He says he thinks we have ley lines under our farmhouse and the farm is really fengshui, with lots of wind and water.

I just need some baling string to connect to the pullets, I mean pulleys. Moon Planet says it's eco-friendly and doesn't harm the environment. Also it needs no fossil fuels and you don't get huge eccentricity bills. Moon Planet connected up the clothes drying apparatus above our old kitchen range. The smell from my drying long johns sure brings a tear to my eye. The other side of my face is wearing a bag of frozen peas. The wife was not impressed and punched me in the eye.

You know when old Mother Riley (Nature?) goes about her daily duties? She doesn't care about straight lines and everything being symmetrical. I mean look at your typical golf course full of people dressed like Rupert Bear, and all the trees planted in a regimental style. To me they don't look right, but our Jenny disagrees (cos she's disagreeable). We are like chalk and chives (cheese is too expensive). Here's a baling string tip for making yourself a plumb line.

32. BALING STRING FOR A PLUMB LINE

The wife thinks different to me about most things. Everything in the house has got to have its own little place and position in the order of things. Personally, I like to take a chaos theory approach to the farm. I can't find a thing when she tidies up.

She decided to do a bit of interior decorating. She wants new wallpaper hanging in the parlour. "There is no special occasion," says I. "It will look like a brothel I once visited in Paris, or was it in Grasmere?"

We set to work clearing the old room. I had awful trouble removing the furze machine from behind the glass cabinet. I did find my old friend Spider though. He's got four wives and they've spun some lovely cobwebs.

The room is finally empty, but it will be the last time I do it. I told the wife about a clever gynaecologist who decorated his house through his letter box. She was not amused and set about looking for a plumb line. I says, "What do you need a plumb line for? We won't hit rocks and be shipwrecked." She

Archie's Top Tip

Don't tie your boot laces
in revolving doors.

smiled and kneed me in my midriff.

It was then that I got the nose bleed and she pushed a bundle of keys down my back on a length of baling string. The keys were cold and ugly, just like the mother in-law. Then she yanked them out and shouted, "Eureka! I've got it." She then used the keys for a plumb line to align the wall paper and set it exactly upright.

It only took four hours to paste and hang the woodchip wall paper. The old farmhouse walls are as straight as a dog's hind legs. The lads must have drunk some BRASSO the day they built our *humble commode.

My mate Mickey went into the local chemist's looking for a potty. The helpful chemist said to Mickey, "I'm very sorry but we don't stock them. Have you tried Boots?" Mickey replied, "Yes but they're no good, it pours out through the laces."

*Ed: humble abode

It's the laces that really bother me. I only get 12 months out of a pair of bootlaces. And look at the price of them. They charge a king's ransom and half a single Farm Payment for them. I will have no more of it, though. Here's a baling string tip for lacing up your boots.

33. BALING STRING FOR LACING UP YOUR BOOTS

I got myself a length of baling string and split it down the middle. I made four pairs of laces and they are as strong as that lad Samson. My only problem is threading them through the eye holes. The wife says that I have got the manual dexterity of a sloth. I thank her for her compliment and ask her to book me an appointment at the opticians. It might cost me money for a new pair of glasses, but at least I won't need to buy bootlaces!

My mate Mickey went into the local chemist's looking for a potty. The helpful chemist said to Mickey, "I'm very sorry but we don't stock them. Have you tried Boots?" Mickey replied, "Yes but they're no good, it pours out through the laces."

I was wondering what to do. Then all of a sudden a light goes on in my head, like whenever I open the fridge door or st Paul's conversion on the road to Domesticity. It was like a miracle. Read on and you can learn how to use baling string for tying up your overcoat too.

34. BALING STRING FOR TYING UP YOUR OVERCOAT

I looks up and sees a large bundle of baling string hanging on a nail. So I puts on the overcoat and ties a length of baling string round me. I dashes into the farmhouse and looks at me'self in the looking glass and decides I look real dapper and dandy. I asked the wife what she thought of my attire. She says, "You look as handsome as Sir John Mills in that film Ryan's Daughter."

The kids of today don't know they're born.
we didn't get to play super Mario games on
our Innuendos and Railway stations. we had
to make our own ways to occupy ourselves.
we used to play knocker a door run, paper
battleships, Japs and Commandoes, Jocks and
Druids and 'Don't Eat That Yellow snow.' Here's a
baling string tip for a rope swing.

35. BALING STRING FOR A ROPE SWING.

The nephew came to see me the other day. He is now a teenager and he doesn't want to go and see the moo cows any more. He says, "Do you mean the cattle?" I decided to pacify the lad and plaited a rope for him out of old baling string. We tied it to the old oak tree in the meadow and attached an old car tyre to it. We had hours of fun on the swing, but I got tired of him saying, "Come on uncle, get off! It's my turn!"

Have you lifted your early
potatoes yet? Don't lift them
in one go or you will need to
wear a truss. Mickey tried shop
lifting. store detectives found him
exhausted underneath Dorothy
Perkins. I don't think she minded
though.

36. BALING STRING FOR TYING UP THE DOORS

The nephew seems to think he is a practical joker. Yesterday morning I gets up and sits on the old lavatory for my morning exercises. I then jumps up from the throne and runs into the kitchen with my trousers round my ankles. I greeted the crowded breakfast table with the immortal words, "Who put clingfilm on top of the toilet?"

Then what does he do when I'm having me nap after breakfast? He only ties all the doors together with my old baling string. I hears a tap on the door and I goes to open it. When I shuts the kitchen door behind me all the doors close. The lad is as daft as a box of frogs!

The wife went to one of those car boot sales the other day and she didn't even need a car boot. She bought an almighty great big painting called the 'Hawaian' by that artist (must be related to a pizza?) John PC Constable.

37. BALING STRING FOR HANGING A PICTURE

It needs a bit of string so that we (me) can hang it. I reluctantly agreed to use some of my baling string. She seems to think I'm made of baling string. I keep telling her it doesn't grow on trees, you know. It's not like I can go to one of them 'ole in the wall' things you see nowadays on the high street and pull another piece out. Mind you them *tree found managers would be better of trading in twine - it always holds its price. Bet we wouldn't be in half the pickle we are in now if they had stuck to string and left those stocks and shares well alone.

*Ed: Hedge Fund Managers?

one of my heifers is sickening for
something, a bit like yours truly and
most sincerely, me! But the missus
won't have any of it. she says
she's too tired of an evening to
tend to a heifer, her verruca veins
and her rhubarb's giving her gip as
well.

38. BALING STRING FOR A LASSO

My heifer is only middling and I decided to bring her home. I
got four lengths of baling string and plaited them into a lasso.
You know, like one of them there ropes with a noose for
catching cattle you see in them cowboy films that we used
to watch on the wireless when we were kids. (My parents
couldn't afford a television.)

I threw my lasso round Buttercup's neck while she grazed
and dreamed of marrying the bull in the field door or farm
gate, if you follow my drift, so to speak.

I grabbed the other end of the rope and she set off like a train
on fire. She dragged me down meadow and dale, through
thistles and furze and nettles, not to mention innumerable
cow pats. I didn't let go, though. I have tamed lions before
today.

Eventually she came to a halt and I brushed myself down
from my bovine saunter. There was nothing wrong with
Buttercup, but I was most annoyed as I had to have a bath.

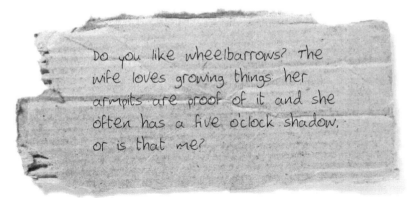

Do you like wheelbarrows? The wife loves growing things her armpits are proof of it and she often has a five o'clock shadow, or is that me?

39. BALING STRING FOR SOWING YOUR VEGETABLE SEEDS

I think it's all down to her age. The doctor prescribed her some of that hormone replacement window's therapy. She tells me that she's going through the change. I said, "It's not just the change, you took a fiver out of my wallet last time I came home drunk."

Besides, the old cake monster seems to be obsessed with growing vegetables. I think she must have been a Town and Country planner in another life, or was she a sewer rat?

Anyway, everything's got to be correctly spaced and she's ever so precise. She often talks about Pythagoras' theory and Einstein's theory about his relatives.

The wife even made me make her a line for sowing the old vegetable seeds. My national collection of baling string is rapidly diminishing by the hour.

I tied two sticks to either end of the string line and the wife sowed an immaculately straight line of carrots. I turned round and admired her garden, which is something I haven't done since our wedding night, at which point I tripped over the line and flew head over heels and my head landed inside a pumpkin.

we are blessed up here in
Lancashire. we are never far
from the sea and the tail end
of the hurricanes in America. still,
it gets rid of the cobwebs in the
breeches, and at least it's always
raining.

40. BALING STRING FOR MAKING A SAIL

The nephew's been pestering me to restore my old fishing boat 'Lazarus' back to life. He wants me to show him how to fish like we did in the old days. If the truth be known, I have never been on a boat in my life. I gets sea-sick if I eat fish and chips!

I try to keep the lad engaged during the long summer holidays. We spent many a grueling five minutes knocking the old girl back into shape. He nailed the planks that he had bought and I straightened the old rusty nails that I provided from an old biscuit tin.

Finally we just needed a mast, a sail and a length of string to tie to the boat sail. The lad says, "Leave it with me," and runs off down the lane, jumping over the hawthorn hedge. The lad's like a young jack rabbit in spring.

I sat down on the overturned hull, lit my pipe and contemplated the meaning of life. I came to the conclusion that it's better to be a barnacle on the ship of life than a badger stuck in a lavatory.

I must have dropped off to sleep when the lad taps me on the shoulder. "Look what I've brought you Uncle Archie." He brandished the wife's clothes prop, her washing line made out of me old baling string and the newly washed eiderdown (my overcoat) complete with the sleeves.

We assembled the sail and threw a tin of Bachelor's peas (on a cord of good old baling string, of course!) at the boat to launch her. "All aboard, all aboard," shouts I and we set sail around the old farm duck pond. Well we were never going on the sea, where we? The wife stood shaking her fists and shouting, "Give me back my washing line."

I have an old cow that must have a bit of the Aborigine in her as she's always going walkabout. I think her father must have belonged to that escapologist Houdini. There's not a field that she can't escape from.

41. BALING STRING FOR TYING A COWBELL ON A COW (FOR OUR AUSTRIAN READERS!)

I even tried using an electric mains fence for the livestock, but I couldn't move the NORWEB electricity pylons. Well you don't think I'm paying for the current myself.

Daisy is a lovely brown and white cow. She wouldn't hurt a fly, but her tail might!

I got me'self one of them cow bells, so I'll be able to hear her when she's grazing the verges round the lanes. The bells are like they have in that Swedish film 'Swedish Erotica.' Or have I got my wires crossed somewhere. I means that Swiss film, 'Heidi.'

The only thing is the bell doesn't have a strap on it, so I'll have to tie some baling string round the cow's neck. I will have to go now and put Daisy in the cattle crush and let the wife wrestle with her!

Do you remember the war when Hitler was going to invade us and drop bombs and shell all the peas. I was staying at my aunt's in sale? They then decided to *emaciate us to a little farm in deepest Lancashire.

42. USING BALING STRING FOR A PARCEL LABEL

My Aunt Patrick (a very strange woman!) wrote and tied a parcel label round my neck with a piece of old baling string. I don't know where she got it from because they still made loose hay in those days.

A tear came to my eye as we boarded the charabanc in Chester that day. I think it must have been the onion I was chewing. My Aunt Patrick tried to calm us all down and told us to be brave in our new home. Then she did the most heroic thing I have ever seen. She knocked on this familiar looking farmhouse door and asked the farmer's wife if she would take us in. My mother clipped me round the ear and said, "I suppose so, but you will have to share your bed with a nun!"

*Ed: Evacuate?

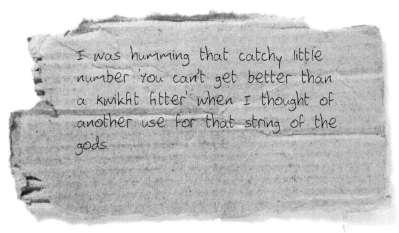

I was humming that catchy little number 'you can't get better than a kwikfit fitter' when I thought of another use for that string of the gods.

43. BALING STRING FOR TYING UP YOUR EXHAUST PIPE

We don't use mechanics were we come from. Let me explain, dear reader. I goes to the town once a week for my pension and to get the shopping. We don't have any of that pubic transport that they have up in the cities. I sometimes thumb a lift, but the last time I stopped a vehicle, I had to sit in the back of the hearse with the coffin. Young Mickey takes me into town on a Friday. He charges me a fiver a mile. The journey's twelve miles, so I give him five pounds and he buys me a pint back. The lad is always prompt to collect me though. I check my watch and he's always half an hour late. He drives an old Robin Reliable. It's only got three wheels. I said he shouldn't be so lazy and should put the spare one on!

The other day we was heading to town and there was this almighty locomotion as the old exhaust decided it'd had enough of this life and threw itself onto the road. There were sparks and banging and I thought we was on the road to Armageddon, or was it Bacup?

Poor old Mickey is an awful flapper, he should have been a Seal. "What will I do, what will I do?" he shouts. "It's a good

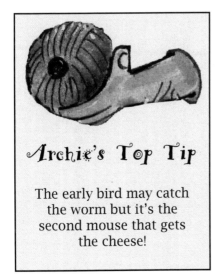

Archie's Top Tip

The early bird may catch
the worm but it's the
second mouse that gets
the cheese!

job I've got my baling string to hold up my trousers," I says.

So Mickey tied up the old exhaust and she was as good as new. We got to town and did the shopping with me clutching on to me breeches, shuffling round the supermarket for dear life like I was one of them Chinamen or was that my cousin Mary? I had to hang on to the breeches though as it's not time to change the long johns for another week or so!

There comes a time in every
marriage when a line must be
drawn in the sand, or to be
more precise, the bedroom. Dear
Mrs Sparrow likes to retire early.

44. BALING STRING FOR SPLITTING UP THE BED

So where do I begin? Scattered about on the bed there's a thermos flask, an old mosquito net, flea powder, cider, Brillo pads, Epsom salts, knitting, lipstick, mascara, a wallpaper scraper, a 'People's Friend' newspaper, the bolster pillow, Mills and Boon books and a box of chocolates with soft centres. They have my teeth marks in them, so I knows they are soft.

I suppose at our time of life we should really have single beds. I mean I haven't crossed 'no man's land' since Sir Alf Ramsey's England side beat Germany. And the wife's always pulling the blankets from under me and her gas mask keeps prodding me in the back.

We have now decided to sign up to a treaty of 'sleep only.' It was her idea mind, not mine, although the thought of seeing us both in our birthday suits doesn't sound that appealing.

I tied a piece of baling string to one end of the iron bedstead. Then I threaded it through the bed linen and tied it to the other iron bedstead. We now sleep in separate areas of the bed. Each one of us has his and her own allotted space to sleep, dream and break wind. She gets the window but I am in charge of the light switch. Not that I am rich enough a farmer to pay for the extravagance of light bulbs!

Me and the lads are having a night out. we've been having a cracking laugh and trying to cadge a few pints from some of them tourists. They say they love 'little old England' and we've shown them a few little old customs!

45. BALING STRING FOR MAKING A BEAUTIFUL BOUQUET FOR THE WIFE

We had one for the road, but it was a very long road so we had another and then we had another one....then I found me'self climbing out of a skip and wondering where the wife was, but I realised I had had too comfortable a night's sleep for me to call it home.

I felt somebody licking my face and I realised that it couldn't be the missus, this creature was much too friendly. It was old Lassie, my faithful black and white hound. She whispered in my ear, "T'is your wedding anniversary so what have you bought her?" I don't know why she speaks with an Irish accent.

Well, I goes all dizzy and my heart beats like one of those kettledrums. I don't know why they should need a cup of tea when they're playing in an orchestra.

I checked my wallet and I only had four fifty pound notes left for medicinal drinks tokens. But in all fairness there aren't many shops open at five in the morning. I mean why is there never a hardware shop open when you need one? I was going to buy her a new mop bucket and a yard brush. I suppose it is the thought that counts!

We finally reached the brow of the hill overlooking our home. I dismounted from Lassie and ran into the farmyard to find some baling string. Then we searched the meadow for some lovely flowers that were in season. It only took a few minutes to make a spray of docks, furze, ragwort and thistles, all tied together with baling string. Well they say 'say it with flowers,' don't they?

I staggered through the farmhouse door and shouted, "Hi honey, I'm home for tea. Happy anniversary my little lotus flower," from the bottom of the stairs. She came down the stairs like that Scarlet O'Hara in 'Gone With The Windows.' She looked positively voluptuous in her donkey jacket. I would have married her again if I had not been married to her already.

I kissed her on the cheek and gave her the flowers. She smacked me over the head with the frying pan.

The nights are closing in now and we go to bed earlier. You can't be burning too much of the eccentric current in these hard times.

46. BALING STRING FOR A CANDLE WICK

Me and the wife have taken to reading for a while. She reads her romances and historical sagas whilst I looks at the pictures in 'Big Girls' Weekly' wrapped up in my old covers of an artificial insemination catalogue from March 1975. She is a little worried as she can't understand why I get so excited.

The wife's been making some of them there candles at her night class. She's trying to educate herself every week. I think she's starting on *electrocution lessons next.

She wanted some money to buy some of them wicks for her candle making activities. I gave her a length of baling string instead. We went to bed early and she attempted to light the baling string candles. The polypropylene baling twine wicks burnt too quickly and quenched like a damp squib.

The wife was not impressed with my saving.

(Ed: elocution?)

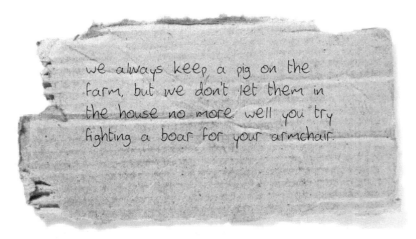

we always keep a pig on the
farm, but we don't let them in
the house no more. well you try
fighting a boar for your armchair.

47. BALING STRING FOR TAKING A PIG TO THE BUTCHER

Well it's time for the pig to go on its final journey. I call the pig Dracula as every time I open the sty door she goes ballistic. She hates the light and won't move. The wife says the pigs have taken after yours truly.

I got a piece of some of my trusted baling string and tied it round her neck. Then we pulled and pushed, but she would not move. I thought of the old adage my father used to say; "You can take a horse to water, but you can't make him drink, or was it think?" He also said the best way to tame a lion is through its stomach. So that night I didn't give her anything to eat, not a sausage!

Next morning I got Mickey to back his car up to the sty and we filled it with cabbage leaves and rolled barley. It looked that good a feast I nearly ate the lot myself!

We used an old tin sheet for a ramp and waited for Dracula to jump in the car for her breakfast. The fat old girl would have none of it though. She was like that cow sitting by the waterside; she would not be moved.

80

We sat in the front of the car wondering what to do. We tapped our fingers on the dashboard and talked about the weather. "A soft day," says Mickey. "I don't know," says me, "We could have one of them earthquakes or hurricanes from America."

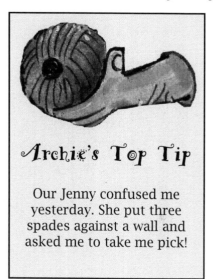

Archie's Top Tip

Our Jenny confused me yesterday. She put three spades against a wall and asked me to take me pick!

All of a sudden there is an almighty whoosh and the car nearly stands up on two wheels. She was like me poor old Ford 3000 tractor when she moves a silage bale. We turned round and looked at what was behind us. My wife's stood there with her sleeves rolled up and mopping her brow. "Right!" says she, "I have thrown the pig in the back. We will take it to the butcher, then we'll do a bit of shopping." Shopping, shopping! I would rather be dropped off with the poor pig!

me and Mickey had a fight last
night. It wasn't over a lass though.
It was much more important than
that. It was about the privatisation
of the water boards.

48. BALING STRING FOR THE BUCKET IN THE WELL

They (whoever they are) are talking about bringing the rates back. I says they should bring back the birch and the blackthorn too. No, seriously, we don't get any services in the countryside, not even church ones, you know. We live in a pineapple republic and just look at the holes in the road. They are like the holes in my socks; they will still be there tomorrow.

We don't have mains water, we have a well and t'is me who carries out the essential maintenance every year. I gets my baling string and plaits a new rope for the 'drawing bucket.'

Here's a meat idea that is better than them posh gizmos that zap the little blighters. I'll give this one to the drago's in that den for nowt.

49. BALING STRING FOR KEEPING THE FLIES AWAY

Do you ever wish you had a tail to flick away the flies. They drive me mad every summer. I think it's the cow dung in the parlour, or is it the wife? I think I will have to get her to dig out the septic tank. It will make good fertiliser for next year's potatoes. Lassie my Heinz 57 hound spends her time trying to catch the flies. I decided to make a fly paper with a piece of parcel paper and some baling string dipped in honey. The honey attracted a swarm of wasps and we are now infested with the blighters. Still, at least it keeps the mother-in-law away!

Doesn't it cost a lot to die these days. when I was younger people could die for far less.

50. BALING STRING FOR MAKING A DIY COFFIN

I am only a poor smallholder and I can't afford to pop my clogs at the moment. My mate Mickey says, "They have never left anybody on the top." Normally he is a few butties short of a picnic, but this time I agree with him.

When Adam was a lad, people used to dig your grave for you and ask your dependents if you wanted to sell your bike. There was always somebody local who could knock you up a coffin out of a old Anderson air raid shelter in exchange for a packet of Victory Vs and a tin of Watney's Pale Ale Party Seven. And whatever happened to Bernie Inns, Caramac chocolate, Spangles and snake belts? They were great, them Bernie Inns. Me and the missus used to go out every Tuesday afternoon and order soup in a basket.

We didn't have funeral directors when I was young. People did it themselves by carrying the coffin on their shoulders, or on the top of a double decker bus if you lived in the other street.

I hear that they are having 'green' funerals nowadays. I reckon that me and Anna Ford, my little Ford 3000 tractor, could save the deceased's family a few bob. There's really no need to make a * Whicker's World coffin.

Here's what I would do for the loved one's family. I would get the missus to empty the tractor's transport box of cow dung. While she's cleaning the hearse (Anna Ford again) I will take Lassie for a walk along the Darwen to Ambleside Ship Canal. I am bound to find some wooden pallets 'chucked in' with all the free newspapers. The pallets will make a lovely cut price coffin and I will use some of my baling string to tie the lid on. With a bit of luck I might find a discarded Asda upermarket trolley. It would be great for carrying the coffin to the graveside. I just hope it doesn't have wonky wheels like yours truly.

*Ed: Does he mean wicker?

They've only gone and sent one of them tax inspectors up to the farm. They say I haven't filled in a tax return for the year 2009. I haven't even filled one in for 1969, never mind 2009.

51. BALING STRING FOR TYING UP THE TAXMAN

They are more nosey than the mother-in-law, if it's possible? Her nickname is The News of The World. She even knows when you went to the toilet last!

The taxman asked me to show him all my farm receipts. I said, "I only deals in cash." Then I asked him if he would like a nice cup of tea. Jenny brewed up (I wish she would keep off them beans) and I said to him, "That will be five pounds, please." Well you don't think he's getting it for nowt, do you?"

The taxman asked more questions than the Gestapo and I started day dreaming. I got some baling string and tied him up into an enormous ball. Then I placed a parcel label on him and posted him to Singapore. Well that's what they'll get when they send anything to yours truly.

This one has been staring me in the face everytime I have ~~sat in my meditation chamber~~ catching up with the news and what that Jordan lass is up to.

Archie's Top Tip

If all the world's a stage, why do all the clowns go in my boozer?

52. BALING STRING FOR TYING UP YOUR TOILET PAPER

You know when I was rabbiting on about them do it yourself coffins? I mentioned the free newspapers that they throw in the local stream. Well I got the wife to wade in and fish them out. We brought four big bundles home in my transport box. We placed them in the barn to dry out and I spent all this morning cutting them into square pieces and making holes in them. I will then thread a long piece of baling string through them. We will have ten years' supply of toilet paper. The wife isn't happy, though. She still wants an inside toilet.

I have said it before and I will say it again: there is no money in small farming. But I have heard that all allotments have waiting lists, so why don't I make one of my fields into allotments. I might make me'self a few bob.

53. BALING STRING FOR PEGGING OUT AN ALLOTMENT

Even Jenny thought this was a good idea so we took a big ball of baling string with us to divide up the allotments. She is ever so pedantic and it wasn't long before we had an argument. To be truthful it wasn't an argument, it was more akin to World War Three.

But Jenny is right. I wish I had never started splitting up the plots. "Left a bit, right a bit." I felt like 'Bernie the Bolt' on that 'Golden Shot' TV programme.

We made twenty thirty by thirty feet allotments. They are known as half plots. Jenny insisted that everything was checked and re-checked a million times. In fairness she made a good job of dividing up the plots. I am now thinking of building a shed and living on one of them; anything to escape from that cake monster Jenny.

I have been thinking about the lack of rural transport in our neck of the woods. It didn't take me long to come up with a solution....

54. BALING STRING TO MAKE YOURSELF A RURAL TAXI

There is more chance of Dick Turpin (his wife Betty makes a lovely hotpot on Coronation Street) giving you a ride home on Black Bess than there is of you getting a taxi home at night. And while we are on the subject of getting about, we don't have any pubic transport either. I am fed up of walking home from my local looking like a drowned rat. I decided to stop moaning and groaning and do 'summat' about it. I have trained our Jenny to drive my little tractor, Anna Ford. I just gives Jenny a blast on the mobile groan and she picks us up from the Dog and Goldfish. We only make her wait three quarters of a hour usually. Well me and my mate Mickey always order three pints each at last orders. Then I buy Jenny a couple of pickled eggs and a bag of pork scratchings as a peace offering. Eventually, after being dragged through the door of the Dog and Goldfish with a shepherd's crook round my neck, me, Lassie (hound and secretary) and Mickey find ourselves standing in the back of the tractor's transport box. Then I attach some baling string reins to the back of Anna Ford. We shout 'Giddy up' and Jenny turns the tractor key. It makes me feel like that Charlton Heston in that film 'Ben Hur.'

Sometimes I have to shout, "Slow down woman!" Well I don't want to lose the wheels off my chariot, do I? Jenny will need the chariot to muck the cows out in the morning.

Brothers, I have a dream.and I went to bed last night and I did have a really strange one. It must have been the pickled eggs I ate last night.

55. BALING STRING TO MAKE A HOMEMADE HANG GLIDER

In my dream I was watching Orville the duck singing "I Wish I Could Fly Right up to the Sky, but I Can't." He is named after one of the Wright brothers, I believe. They were entrepreneurs, publishers and bicycle manufacturers. They were a bit like me; self-taught geniuses.

Orville and Wilbur observed the way birds fly and manoeuvre on the wing. I often study the birds myself. But Jenny won't let me buy that newspaper with the page 3 section in it any more. But I woke up with a brilliant idea; I was going to make a hang-glider.

I belong to the old school of 'if in doubt, give it a clout.' It always works when the telly starts playing up. Anyway, I dreamed that we made a hang glider with some of my baling string. Myself and Mickey went round the town collecting four wooden clothes props. We didn't steal them, we just borrowed them on a permanent basis. Then I got some old plastic pit silage covers and tied them to the frame with baling string. She looked a right bobby dazzler of a hang glider. I'd like to do some hand gliding with Tracey, the buxom barmaid in the Dog and Goldfish.

Me and Mickey are taking the hang glider to Wigan tomorrow. I hear that they have a lovely pier where we can launch her.

As you will know by now I am totally PC and any meetings held about my allotments will be completely democractic....

56. BALING STRING FOR A LIMBO LINE

My allotments have new tenants. We decided to hold a meeting tonight in my barn. It was totally democratic. "What I says goes." We don't allow any man-made chemicals whatsoever. We are going to apply for orgasmic certification. I chaired the first meeting by saying, "If you don't adhere to my rules, I will set the wife on you."

Anyway, there is a new lad originally from Jamaica called Winston. He says he is going to grow chickens and sweet potatoes. Winston likes drinking Caribbean Bacardi and he said we should 'cool down and chill.' Winston is full of brilliant ideas and he is being appointed concert secretary for our allotments society. He says that back in Jamaica when they have a party they all limbo dance to 'break the ice.'

Jenny reckons I actually invented limbo dancing when I had to use a pay toilet in the Winter Gardens in Blackpool.

We had a great time drinking Caribbean Bacardi. I rummaged round the back of my barn and I extracted two council traffic cones that I found in my local shop, the canal. Then we tied a piece of baling string in between them and 'limboed.' 'Tracey' the buxom barmaid from the Dog and Goldfish won first prize and had to repeat her performance several times.

I'll give this idea for free to the management at the Royal Mail as we keep hearing all the time that they need a bit of good news (but all they ever seem to bring me is bills).

57. BALING STRING TO FIX UP A POST BOX

The new allotment society is taking up a lot of my time. Lassie is the new secretary and she composts all the letters. We have also made a letterbox from an old ten gallon drum. I cut a slot in it and tied it with baling string to the old horse chestnut tree. I just hope we have a better postal service than our postman Tommy. He is that bloody slow and the dog won't let him near the farmhouse. Or is that the mother-in-law?

Ed: compiles?

we are getting a right
cosmopolitan ~~feet~~ to our new
~~allotments~~. An ~~Australian lad's just~~
took one of the plots. He reminds
me of that Mick Dundee in
'Crocodile Dundee'.

58. BALING STRING FOR A CORK HAT

Wally is a bit naïve and gets on the bus and stands at the front talking to the bus driver. At least he isn't as bad as the characters that I used to meet on the bus. Once I was sat on my own on the top deck of an empty bus going to Oldham. This gentleman (a nutter) then comes and sits himself next to me and says, "Is there anybody sat next to you?" He then sadly, I might say, gave me an oration at the top of his voice which went, "Onward Christian Soldiers, Marching on to War." Laugh, I nearly got my cigs out!

Where was I? (On the bus!) No seriously. Wally Dingo is a new Australian tenant on my allotments. He recently gave me an idea for my baling string. The flies and insects have really been annoying me lately and I wish I had a tail like Lassie or one of my cows. Well, I do have a sort of tail, but I'm not allowed to wave it about.

Anyway, the wasps and fruit flies have really been bothering me. It is a sorry state of play when you can't sit on your deckchair supping cans of beer whilst the missus digs your allotment free from interruption by insects.

93

I mentioned my insect predicament to Wally. He said that he had just the ticket. Back home in Australia they use corks hung from hats to ward off insects and crocodiles and he says he will make me a hat to ward off the insects. I am providing the baling string and he is providing the wine bottles for the corks! We spent all last night singing, "Tie me Kangaroo down (with baling string!), Sport."

The new allotments are looking
great. They are a real hive of
activity. I like to 'talk' a good
allotment. My war wounds won't
allow me to do any manual work.
Jenny says that I think manual
labour is a spanish footballer!

9. BALING STRING FOR FINDING YOUR GARDEN TOOLS.

My point is this: why do gardening tool manufacturers paint everything flipping green? Yes, I know it's mother nature's favourite colour, but that doesn't mean much when you're thrashing about like a fish out of water on your jungle of an allotment, looking for your garden shears.

I don't know, it's a mixed up world. I will give you an example. Last week we went to Manchester to do some Christmas shopping. We walked round one of those enormous department stores where the customer assistants say in a Dalek like voice, "Can I help you?" I got right confused when I wandered off on my own. One door said 'PULL,' so I pulled it. Another door said 'PUSH,' so I pushed it. I then walked up to this other door and it said 'LIFT.' I only goes and traps me fingers.

I have now come to the conclusion that the best way to find your gardening tools is to do the following; get yourself some shocking pink paint and some large lengths of baling string. Then paint your tools and tie big loops of baling string on them. You could even tie them to lumps of concrete or to

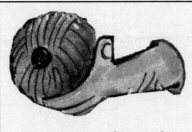

Archie's Top Tip

There was a great loss recently. The bloke who wrote the "Hokey Pokey," song died. It was extremely difficult for the undertaker to get him in the coffin. They put his left leg in...

your allotment slave, ie. the wife. (By the way, I am not sexist! If the wife wants to be a feminist, that's fine by me. She can do whatever she wants as long as the cows and pigs are mucked out and my tea is on the table. Think on, tool manufacturers. Shocking pink paint and baling string!

Dear reader, I often hark back to when things were a lot easier, when you didn't need washing machines and all these fancy gizmos for doing the simplest of jobs, just a devoted wife.

60. BALING STRING FOR PATCHING UP YOUR LONG JOHNS

The wife wants a new washing machine. She says I can use the old dolly tub to grow my carrots in. It will keep away the carrot fly because they don't fly above 14 inches. It sounds like a fair idea. Jenny keeps to the same washing routine every Monday morning, come rain or shine. Then she hangs all our underwear out for the neighbours to see. I've noticed that the long johns need a bit of darning work. I have only had them twenty two years. You can't get any proper cotton anymore. Well not since they made the local mill into a lap dancing club. Jenny says she's found a novel way of repairing my underwear. She says she is going to darn them with some of my baling string.

The wife's gone to one of her 'WELL WOMAN, PIG REARING AND FLAT PACK FURNITURE ASSEMBLY COURSES.' she'll come back full of self-help nonsense but what use is it without baling string?

61. BALING STRING FOR WASHING A PAN

The course is in Halifax. I don't think she will like the foreign grub. Well, it's in Yorkshire, isn't it? I am having to feed myself. Our Lassie is hopeless at cooking baked beans. Her paws can't use the tin opener properly. Mostly I dine out at the Dog and Goldfish. Tracey makes some lovely pickled egg and Branston sandwiches. I asked Tracey to get me a packet of helicopter crisps. She said, "Sorry Archie, we've only got plain ones." She is not the sharpest pencil in the pencil case, but when she bent down for the ready salted crisps.... Well! Dear reader, it made an old man happy!

I have been in a right predicament (or pickle, if you're one of the eggs in my local boozer). Didn't I come home from the pub yesterday afternoon? I had only had ten pints and four double whiskies. I gets in our house and I feels like one of my hens; very peckish. So I bangs a tin of baked beans on the cooker.

I then fell asleep watching 'Upstairs Downstairs' on the wireless. They don't show it on television anymore. The beans were suddenly as black as the Ace of Spades. Worse still I'd blackened a pan belonging to Jenny. I got Lassie to lick it but it didn't remove the mark. Then I had one of my brainwaves and I made a scouring pad out of scrunched up baling string. It worked a treat. I have also found a new way of washing up. I put the plates on the floor for our Lassie to lick. Who needs washing up liquid?

Jenny saw a rat run across one of the allotments. Then she said she had seen 'him' again. I tried to explain that the rat would not be the same rat. she would have seen several rats. Jenny was adamant though that it was the 'same lad'

62. BALING STRING FOR A BOW AND ARROW

It looks like we are in the midst of an *epidural, I have been busy making a bow and arrow to kill these rodents. An old willow branch and some baling string is all you need. Well I don't like using poison and I keep standing on the traps.

We waited all night (five minutes) for one of the 'lads' to appear. They never surfaced though. I have hung a photograph of the mother-in-law on the gate. One look at that picture and the rats will never be seen again.

* Ed: epidemic

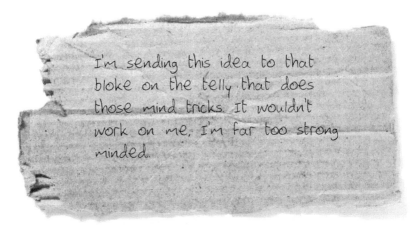

I'm sending this idea to that bloke on the telly that does those mind tricks. It wouldn't work on me, I'm far too strong minded.

63. BALING STRING FOR A ROPE TRICK

There's a new bloke just rented one of my allotments. He's called Ali and he was born in India. He says he wants to grow lots of Asian spices for his curries. He also cuts hair for a living. We call him Ali Barber. He's also a part-time magician.

I asked if he knew of any magic tricks to entertain us. Ali told us about the Indian rope trick. It was supposed to be performed out on the streets of India in the 1850s. One of the Fakirs would throw a rope in the air. (I am not swearing, I said Fakir!) Then a small boy would climb up the rope and disappear. Rather like Jenny when it's time to get a round of drinks in.

Ali gave me an idea. I could get out some of my baling string and perform my own rope trick. The only thing is I need summat to keep it erect. I know what I will do. I will send Mickey round to Boots the chemist. I think they sell Viagra over the counter. Jenny says I should get some for myself as well!

Ed: Does he mean pig ignorant

I like to think of myself as one of them new men. My misses often says she would like a new man so it would make her happy too!

64. BALING STRING FOR A G STRING

A funny thing happened to me the other night. I walked into the snug of the Dog and Goldfish. I forgot it was the ladies' darts team and cinema hoovering club. They were having an Ann Summers exotic lingerie evening. The things I saw. They made me blush like one of the beetroots on our allotments. The girls were giggling and laughing and I just sat down and ordered a pint of mixed.

I'm a man of the world and like me dear old father used to say, "Don't be shy; your mother wasn't." Well that's what I thought, but then you know what happens? Tracey the voluptuous bar maid comes in wearing some sexy laundry looking like one of them air-raid sirens that lured the sailors.

But Tracey gave me an idea. I supped ten more pints and waited for Donna Summer to turn up and do some singing, but she never turned up. I then crawled home and made Jenny a G string out of some of my old baling string. It was such an obvious use for it! I can't wait to give her my birthday present.

we are having a fancy dress do down at the Dog and Goldfish tonight. I wanted to go on my knees dressed as a small farmer, but Jenny said that would be too boring. what's boring about being a small farmer?

65. BALING STRING FOR A MEXICAN BANDIT MOUSTACHE

We always have interesting things to talk about. We talk about the price of cattle, the price of sheep, the price of tractor diesel, the price of silage, the price of hay, the price of pigs, the price of a pint of beer, the price of eggs, the price of meat, the price of coal, the price of fertiliser, the price of hen food, the price of beef nuts, the price of ginger nuts, the price of bread and the price of keeping a wife. Oh, I forgot something else; the price of electricity and toilet paper. We also like to talk about the weather. If it's too hot there will be no grass. If it's too wet we will have no hay. If it's too cold my tractor won't start. If it's summer it will be too light and I won't be able to sleep, but if it's winter it will be too dark and I will have to put the light on. It's an awful dilemma being a farmer.

At least I am not a woman farmer though. They are like a cow and a calf. Have you heard them rabbiting in the market. I can't be doing with their *conservations. It's always, "Eggs, lettuce, new shoes. How's Mrs Bradshaw and the new baby? Eggs, lettuce, new shoes."

Anyhow, to cut a long story short, I have been watching them Ravioli Westerns with Clint Eastwood. He doesn't mess about. I think I will get myself a blunderbuss and fill it with bacon rind. Then I will get some baling string and some more of my plumbers glue and I will make one of them Mexican Bandit Moustaches. I will also need a sombrero and a poncho for me back.

I can't wait for any double grazing salesmen, politicians or trespassers to saunter up my fields. I will just shout, "Hey Gringo!" and give their backsides a pelting with bacon rind.

Ed: conservations

I love weddings - it's the only time I get to have rice with me tea!

66. BALING STRING FOR TYING THINGS TO THE WEDDING CAR

The niece is getting married a week on Saturday. She is a nice lass but she's got more front than Blackpool promenade. They have sent us one of them wedding lists. Everything has to come from a posh department store in Manchester. There is no such thing as a toast rack and a pair of bicycle clips like when we got married. I don't know why they are bothering getting wed. If I was them I would live over the brush or the vacuum cleaner to be modern. When me and Jenny first got wed we lived over a chippy in a flat.

They have not even invited me to the do in the town hall. I didn't want to go any road. I would much rather go to a funeral - you don't need to take a present.

I have decided to give them a great sending off present. Me and Mickey are going to have a right good tidy up. Not us personally, I am talking about around the farm. We are going to get some baling string and tie all the old paint tins, buckets, beer cans and whatever to the bride and bridegroom's car. Well, it's a cheap way of getting rid of your rubbish and they can't say I didn't give them 'owt.

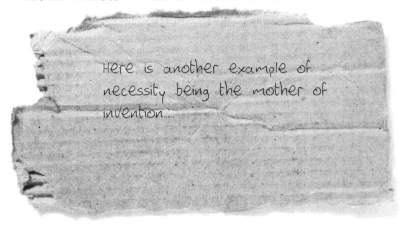

Here is another example of necessity being the mother of invention.....

67. BALING STRING FOR A STRING SHOPPING BAG

I see yon government in London might be introducing a levy for them plastic carrier bags. They'll charge you ten pence and then they'll expect you to walk around advertising their store. Why don't they just give you a sandwich board and ask you to walk up and down the high street.

Archie's Top Tip

I have a balanced attitude to drinking - I hold a beer in each hand.

Any road, they won't make Archie Sparrow pay. I have just the ticket. I will get the wife to knit me a baling string shopping bag. It'll be just like the vest but without the arm and neck holes!

Bloody hell! The cat's really pissed on the chips now. Mollie (Lassie) informs me that it is the wife's birthday. I haven't bought her 'owt.

68. BALING STRING TO MAKE A STANDARD LAMP

I have had one of me microwaves again. Jenny once told me that she would like the best room in our house to be like one of them like you see on Steptoe and Son, or was it Dynasty? You know, they always have fruit in a bowl on the sideboard, even when nobody's ill.

Jenny says that she would like one of them Standard Liège lamps. But shush! I have got to be quiet. I am in the front room stood on the mop bucket and holding a council warning flash light wearing my baling string cork hat. I hope Jenny likes her new baling string standard lamp.

* Ed: brain waves

some of you, even this far into my little book, will still deny the usefulness of baling string. well read on and prepare to admit defeat in the face of a superior mind

69. BALING STRING FOR HOLDING UP YOUR CHRISTMAS CARDS

I told you about us decorating the best room, didn't I? Well me and Jenny have been having a heated discussion about Christmas cards. She wants me to put her up a line to hang them on. But since it is newly decorated she won't allow me to use nails or drawing pins. She says we have to get some bluetack thingumajig kind of tackle. It's apparently a bit like plasticine, but it doesn't taste as good.

Any road, I got some of my baling string and made her a line. The cards look great, but a bit skew whiff due to all the knots. We then had an argument about who got the most Christmas cards. Jenny seems to get the most. I wish the senders would write their names in pencil, then I could rub them out and send them back as part of my recycling. The only trouble is I would have to buy a rubber. Awfully costly, what? There are some things baling string just cannot do!

The wife threw me out last night.
I am now homeless and living
in the shed she didn't like my
birthday present. I said it's the
thought that counts and she said
that's exactly the problem!

70. BALING STRING FOR A BRAZIER

It is the middle of winter and I have been locked out of my own home by the evil cake monster! What makes it worse is she has used some of my baling string to tie up the doors. Oh, what amusement it gave the allotment holders as I picked up all my clothes off the main road.

I have made me'self a brazier out of an old oil barrel and filled it with hay and some of my old baling string. I couldn't get it going though, so I decided to throw a bit of petrol on it. The whole thing went whoosh and now I haven't got any eyebrows. I am going to get some baling string and glue and make some new ones. I reckon I will look like that Omar Sharif fellow.

All this talk of braziers makes me wonder if there are any other items of lingerie I could make.

I find I am continually observing things in the school of life. For example, I don't know why but all bus drivers read the Daily Mirror. Did you realise that socialists were driving you round?

71. BALING STRING TO STOP YOU LOSING YOUR PENS OR PENCILS

I was in the butchers the other day asking for a sheep's head with the legs left on and I noticed old Mr Angus (he does come from Aberdeen) had a pencil behind his ear.

It was then that I had both a sudden bowel movement and a rather profound question to ask him. I leaned on the counter and said, "Why do they put rubbers on pencils, Mr Aberdeen? He smiled and said, "Because everybody makes mistakes, Archie." The butcher is right and I have decided to do something about the matter. I have asked Jenny for a reconciliation: I want to come back home. She said she will think about it.

In the meantime I have got myself a two hundred and twenty foot long length of baling string and tied it to my pen. Well, I can never find one when I am on the phone in the village telephone kiosk. You don't think I am going to have one installed in the farmhouse do you? It costs far too much.

Did I tell you about a drunk accosting me last week? He said, "Excuse me, mate, can you tell me where the other side of the road is?" I said, "It's over there lad." The drunk just shook his head and said, "some daft fool just told me it was over here!"

72. BALING STRING TO OFFICIALLY OPEN YOUR OLD HOME

Lassie brought me an envelope this morning. It was a letter for me from Jenny. I asked Lassie to read it for me. I am *illegitimate, you see. Lassie had to go back to the farmhouse for her reading glasses. Dogs don't eat carrots as a rule, but they should, you know. You never see rabbits wearing glasses and they eat tons of carrots, don't they?

Lassie read out the letter. It's a shame I have never learned "Woof, woof." Luckily she knows a bit of English so she could read out Jenny's new farmhouse rules that she wanted me to agree to if I was to come back. They were:

1. No breaking wind and saying 'new shoes, Vicar'

2. No lying in bed and expecting room service

* Ed: illiterate

3. No eyeing up that barmaid Tracey and talking about her in your sleep

4. No conjugal rights unless you win the lottery (or a five minute trolley dash in netto)

5. No coal in the bath

6. No breaking up the internal doors for firewood because you can't be bothered going outside as it's raining

7. No cutting your toe nails with the bread knife

8. No holding on to the television remote control and hiding it under your cushion

9. No tractor parts or baling string to be allowed in the confines of the bedroom

10. No doing anything without first asking Jenny Sparrow

Signed this day

Archie sparrow

Archie Sparrow

It is coming to something when an Englishman's castle is actually his garden shed. I have reluctantly agreed to sign Jenny's charter. Anything is better than living in a shed with a spider called Sid and a rucksack full of Rolf Harris stylophones from a car boot sale job lot in Helmshore (or was it Wadebridge?) for a pillow.

Jenny tied a piece of baling string across the threshold, then she cut it and welcomed me to my 'new home.' She had also placed an 'UNDER NEW MANAGEMENT' sign in the farmhouse window for everyone to see.

There's some ignorant people who reckon that men's football is better than women's. They have much to learn.

73. BALING STRING FOR PATCHING UP A GOAL NET

Tracey the barmaid has started a ladies' football team. They play down at the local park. I went to watch them and give them some of my worldly advice; "If in doubt, kick it out and give it some welly and clog-pie." They are not bad and I hope they get to the cup final. Well, the players always swap shirts at the end of a cup final.

I am a hero in the eyes of the Dog and Goldfish ladies' football team. Every time they bang a goal in the back of the net the ball squeezes through and ends up in the river. I soon came to the rescue with twenty five feet of my baling string. All the girls hugged and kissed me. I felt like that *Hugh Heifer who owned that Playboy mansion. The girls think that I am awfully clever. Well, I did used to be a deep sea trawler fisherman on the Leeds to Liverpool canal.

*Ed: Hugh Hefner

I'm a great one for cutting down me carbon 'footstep' and reckon that Greenpeace will be wanting to hear this idea of mine.

74. BALING STRING FOR A TOW ROPE

Hello comrades. Me and Mickey went out for a drive in his Robin Unreliable yesterday. It's great to get away from the smallholding and Jenny for a while. We were going to have a look round Southport sewage treatment works, but it was closed due to it being a Sunday. We stopped in Tarleton and bought a bag of chips between us.

On the way back home Mickey said, "We will have to get some petrol." I decided to put plan 678b into place. There was no way I was using my beer tokens to pay for petrol. We popped into a nice little pub and had a drink instead. Then we got out some of my baling string and tied it to the front bumper and to Mickey's waist. I sat in the driver's seat and shouted, "Pull!" It was not long before passing motorists saw our predicament. A kind policeman offered to tow us home. I thanked him profusely and offered him some of my green and yellow midget gems. Well, you want the red and black ones for yourself, don't you!

So, ladies and gentlemen, if you want to save money and petrol, make yourself a baling string towrope. You will cut down your carbon footprint and save yourself a few bob for a few slurps.

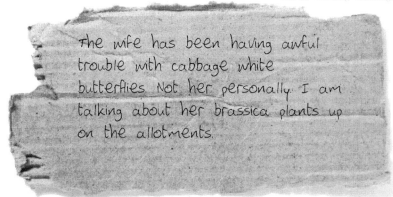

The wife has been having awful trouble with cabbage white butterflies. Not her personally. I am talking about her brassica plants up on the allotments.

75. A BALING STRING NET FOR CATCHING CABBAGE WHITE BUTTERFLIES

Her cabbages resemble our net curtains, except the cabbages don't need washing and they don't move when somebody walks down the road.

We have tried all sorts of methods but none of them seems to work. I even tried warm, soapy water, but I didn't like it. It made me think of having a bath: I am not due one until next September. Jenny said that we should share a romantic bath together. I would rather share a Pot Noodle with the Loch Ness monster!

Archie's Top Tip
If you fall and break your legs don't coming running to me

I am busy supervising Jenny as she knits herself a cabbage white net out of some of my old baling string; "Knit one, pearl one, boil in the bag, eat a banana, knit one, pearl one...."

The great outdoors - loads better than the great her indoors anyday!

76. BALING STRING FOR GUY ROPES

Do you know Guy Ropes? No, he is not related to Guy Fawkes. I am talking about them things that they stick on the front of tents.

Do you remember that hippy lad Moon Planet (Wayne) who gave me a clothes airer? Well he's been telling me about them festivals they have in summer seat or is it Somerset? You know, the one where Lily Allen dances round the stage wearing a purple rinse. It's hardly original as our post office is always full of purple rinses on pension day.

But talking about colours, Moon Planet says that when he goes to Glastonbury people are always tripping over his guy ropes and snapping them. He says it's because they eat too many Wine Gums and drink too much 7UP. (More like they are stoned and been on the Wacky Baccy (or cannibal plants). You can't pull the baling string over my eyes.

Any road, I think I have come up with a saline solution. We are going to start tie dyeing baling string and making festival guy ropes. I could be the next Richard Branston.

116

Me and Moonbeam got arrested last night. All we were doing was trying to catch pink and yellow elephants in the ladies' underwear department in Marks and Spencer's. What's wrong with that?

77. BALING STRING FOR CATCHING PINK AND YELLOW ELEPHANTS

I had a go on Moonbeam's bong last night. He made it out of an old milk bottle. It reminds me of one of those hookahs that they have in that film the '39 Stepladders.' It was rather refreshing and I felt a wonderful sense of peace and enlightenment. Moonbeam told me that he had just seen a tartan giraffe looking through the window. I didn't see any tartan giraffes, but I did see a pink and yellow elephant on the loose.

I quickly made myself an elephant net. I will never forget that Blue Peter television programme with the young elephant when Valerie Simpleton was incredibly *indigenous. She used to show you how to make your very own nuclear fallout shelter from two PG Tips tea bags, a packet of Paxo stuffing, an old Ski yoghurt carton and some sticky back plastic (I don't know why she didn't realise it was Sellotape, everybody else did!).

*Ed: ingenious

The nephew is sixteen today. He wants a moped for his birthday. He wants his own wheels and freedom. when I was a lad we used to get around on 'shanks's pony.'

78. BALING STRING FOR A MOPED MOP HEAD

Jenny says we will have to have a whip round. I think there might be some pre-decimation coins in the gas meter. I was saving them for the collection at the church at Harvest Festival.

Then I had an idea. The lad apparently wants a mophead (moped) so he will get one. I got the old mop handle and nailed twenty baling string strands to it. The nephew is now the very proud owner of his own mop head.

*Ed: pre-decimalization

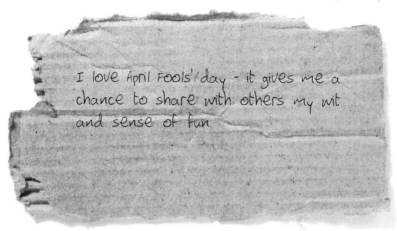

I love April Fools' day - it gives me a chance to share with others my wit and sense of fun.

79. BALING STRING FOR GROWING EXOTIC VEGETABLES

The new allotments are really buzzing. They are a credit to all the tenants. They are growing all sorts of *erotic vegetables. They are growing potatoes, sweet potatoes, onions, lettuces, radishes, red hot chilli peppers (I thought they were a rock group?), marrows, aubergines, Jerusalem artichokes, cabbages, parsnips, yams, kohlrabi (doesn't he work in a synagogue), leeks, beetroots, Swedes, celery.... you name it, they are growing it.

I have decided to show them how to grow something really erotic. I have covered an old Salix (willow tree) with lengths of baling string and empty tin cans and have told the allotment holders that I am growing my own spaghetti.

*Ed: exotic

119

once again I've got an idea that Greenpeace will love. It doesn't need batteries or electricity.

80. BALING STRING FOR A KNOCKER UPPER

Do you have an alarm clock? We couldn't afford one when I was young. We used to pay old Jimmy Entwistle a penny a week to tap on the upstairs window with a large bamboo pole. Jimmy was called the knocker upper. No, he didn't go round putting young lasses in the family way.

You could make your own alarm clock by tying a thirty foot length of 'guess what' to your big toe. Then thread it through the sash windows and let it drop to the floor. Arrange with an early bird to come around at your agreed waking time. Then tell them to give the baling string a tug. Hey presto, you have your very own baling string alarm clock.

You can always rely on Archie Sparrow to show you how to save a few bob.

121

what do you reckon to them
tea bags with the string attached
They are awfully expensive. I
have decided to make my own
stringed tea bags. shall I let you
into my secret?

81. BALING STRING FOR A TEA BAG

Get yourself some muslin material. The gusset of the wife's drawers will do (you wouldn't want mine). Do you realise I have just invented the first crotch-less long johns?

Now make the muslin into a bag and fill it with tea or sawdust if it's for the tax inspector. Now tie a piece of old baling string to the bag and you have a state of the art tea bag.

If you're lucky enough to have a hot water tap, fill up your cup and put your home-made tea bag in the cup. Now put some cow's milk in and give it to the wife. Well she can't say I never made her a 'nice cup of tea.'

They reckon that you can get five cups of tea from a tea bag. What a waste! I can get at least fifty five cups of tea from one of mine.

THE END

A Note from the Author

My childhood holidays were always spent on my grandparents' farm in Southern Ireland (except on the odd occasion when we went to Scarborough). It was a nostalgic time and the haymaking left a great impression on me.

Let me take you back to 1968..............

The Beatles had just formed their soon to be world famous Apple record label. On May 29th 1968 George Best and his comrades (better known as Manchester United) had just destroyed the mighty and great Eusebio's Benfica at Wembley stadium.

Two months later and just ten miles away from Manchester my father would be given his two weeks "wakes" holidays from his job in a Lancashire woollen felt mill. The journey to his parents seemed like an epic voyage. We would travel by bus, train, ferry, bus again and finally by car the last few miles to the farm. Today a person could fly to Australia in the same time, but only if they had an aeroplane!

The journey was always tiresome and seemed never ending to me as a small child of five. We travelled from Heuston train station in Dublin down to Cork City. The train hurtled through fields full of cattle, sheep, vegetables and hay. Farmers stayed at home tending their mist encircled, apple shaped hills. Ireland seemed a rural paradise back then and everybody seemed happy. My neighbour's mother would always say, "Be poor and be happy." The small farmer seemed self-sufficient.

We departed the train at Cork City and boarded the C.I.E. bus (the one with the red setter picture on its side) and travelled the last sixty miles down to West Cork. We often shared the bus with nuns and farmers and their wives clutching crates of live hens and ducks. Foreign tourists carried rucksacks, tents and clumsy looking bicycles. A proverbial drunk was often part of the travelling furniture and he would usually provide the entertainment.

We finally arrived in my father's home town and we would go in a bar frequented by my ancestors for the last hundred years or more. I wouldn't like the drinks bill.

"Welcome home boy" said the lads at the bar to my father as they raised their pints of Beamish, Smithwicks, and Guinness. They would all be dressed in their unofficial West Cork rural farm uniforms of tweed jackets, old suit trousers and the essential cloth cap. It was a scene similar to the characters from any Lowry painting back in Salford.

It was a strange pub compared to the pubs back in England. You walked through the pub door and you found yourself in a grocer's shop. Behind the grocer's there was a little 'snug bar' for the women to have a drink and mind the children where hopefully she would not be accosted by some 'drunken, smelly farmer.' Behind the 'snug' there was a large public bar, mainly for the men folk. It had a long bar with a few tables and chairs, all hard as church pews. Outside in the back yard there was a gents' toilet with a solitary cold tap. At the far end of the yard there was a blacksmith's forge. The bar was perfect if you wanted to have your horse shoed, go to the toilet, have a few slurps, meet the wife and order your week's shopping while you got drunk. You can't do that in Tesco's!

We would then attempt to get a taxi out to my grandparents' farm. A hackney carriage in those days was as rare as rocking horse droppings. Eventually we would cadge a lift along the winding road to my grandparents.

The car finally screeched to a halt and there before my eyes stood my grandparents and my uncle Bill. Teddy the red and white sheepdog barked and jumped and licked us to death. We exchanged gifts and hugs and my father was treated like the returning prodigal son.

Next day, to use a Lancashire saying, 'the sun would be cracking the flags.' We would get up and help milk the seven Friesian cows and Uncle Bill would sit on a stool singing, "You can pull my hair and you can pull my tail but I won't get up in the morning."

After breakfast it would be time to dress the horse. Uncle Bill would bring Paddy to the cart house to get ready for work. The horse was a great big grey fellow who one year was called Charlie and the next he was called Paddy Boy. He was a large speckled carthorse with the temperament of a neurotic psychopath. Often Uncle Bill would place large manacles on his back legs to stop him jumping over the fuchsia hedge and running down the borreen to town. The horse was like a puppy when my grandmother Elizabeth went in the field and stroked him. "Aren't ye a nice fellow, Paddy Boy," she would say. The horse would neigh and whimper and droop his ears. Paddy was always good with me and he would let me ride bareback using his mane for reins. We would dress the horse and Uncle Bill would say "Now, t'is time for Paddy to put his clothes on. He would place the harness and britchin on Paddy's back and say, "These are his braces," then he would place the collar around the horse's neck and say, "This is his shirt."

The horse would then be attached to the cart with rubber car tyres and we'd set off to gather the newly mown loose hay. My father, my grandfather, Uncle Bill and the neighbours would toil in the hot summer, raking and piking the new hay onto the cart. It was a joy to run amongst the windrows while the sun made us brown as berries.

Rabbits used to sit and watch the hay being harvested. They watched knowingly like old farmers thinking "they're nothing but greenhorns, they're not doing it right."

It was thirsty work and my mother and grandmother would fetch us bottles of cold tea wrapped in an old sock, which remarkably quenched our thirst. When the cart was full we would jump on top of the precariously overflowing hay and the horse would wearily tread the half mile home. Many were the times we would duck our heads under the low overhead electricity cables. Oh what fun to be a small boy. They were wonderful times, now gone forever to be replaced with silage.

ARCHIE SPARROW'S BOOK OF USEFUL TIPS.....

Back home in England we lived close to a farm and I often helped them with the hay bale gathering. One of my friends worked for a fortnight for a tight old farmer who rewarded him for his work with a 'Penguin' chocolate biscuit for wages. I have met many more 'mean' or should I perhaps say 'careful' farmers since then and I find myself now having something of a Heath Robinson approach to fixing things and making do.

Now all these years later I live on a small farm in the Republic of Ireland. I also own a little Ford 3000 tractor. I bought her brand new when she was 30 years old. At the time of writing she is being used for mucking out and lifting silage bales (often on two wheels). I dis name her Anna after the BBC newsreader and because she's a Ford.

Perhaps I will write a book about my little tractor and her many humorous uses some day? I dedicate this book to my family and to all who struggle farming and tending allotments.

I have heard that in China everybody is allotted a piece of land to grow your own vegetables. It's a shame that we are not made to do the same.

I am also led to believe that if you get sterilized (not the milk), the government will give you a free transistor radio. I wouldn't be sterilised for a wireless, although Archie might be tempted if they threw a couple of drinks in too, but if they offered me broadband I would seriously think about it!

Here's power to your pikes and garden forks!

DAVE DEALY.

ANY FOOL CAN BE.....A DAIRY FARMER
By James Robertson

James Robertson set out for the beautiful, badger-haunted fields of Devon to turn grass into gold via the medium of milk. It only took an encounter with his first cow to realise that he would need the survival instincts of the SAS if he were to live to appreciate this rural idyll.

His cows did not seem to live up to their public image of placid benevolence and created a working environment as ruthless as that of the London advertising agency from which he had escaped. There were cows with sharpshooter hooves, an amorous bull set on enjoying the favours of a neighbour's herd - or even those of the farmer himself, should he turn his back - and the terrible tyranny of a newborn calf.

ISBN 9781904871729

ANY FOOL CAN BE A.....PIG FARMER
By James Robertson

This, the first of James Robertson's sagas about agriculture and country life, demonstrates that the young and inexperienced Robertson was even move prone to disaster than the older and still inexperienced Robertson. His pigs bit him, gave him lice, crawled up to his bed and indicated that man is not necessarily the dominant species.

How do you communicate the facts of life to an innocent young boar, persuade a sow not to eat her young, survive an investigation by the Inland Revenue and stay out of jail when your newly insured barn goes up in smoke?

Set amid the picturesque slag heaps of the North Wales border region, Any Fool Can Be a.....Pig Farmer shows the other side of the rural idyll. It is painful, real and very funny.

ISBN 9781904871712

The Good Life Press Ltd.
The Old Pigsties
Clifton Fields
Lytham Road
Preston PR4 0XG
01772 633444

The Good Life Press Ltd. publishes a wide range of titles for the smallholder, 'goodlifer' and farmer. We also publish **Home Farmer,** the monthly magazine for anyone who wants to grab a slice of the good life - whether they live in the country or the city. Other titles of interest include:

A Guide to Traditional Pig Keeping by Carol Harris
An Introduction to Keeping Cattle by Peter King
An Introduction to Keeping Sheep by J. Upton/D. Soden
Any Fool Can Be....a Middle Aged Downshifter by Mike Woolnough
Build It! by Joe Jacobs
Build It!....With Pallets by Joe Jacobs
Craft Cider Making by Andrew Lea
Flowerpot Farming by Jayne Neville
Making Country Wines, Ales and Cordials by Brian Tucker
Making Jams and Preserves by Diana Sutton
No Time to Grow by Tim Wootton
Precycle! by Paul Peacock
Raising Chickens by Mike Woolnough
Raising Goats by Felicity Stockwell
The A-Z of Companion Planting by Jayne Neville
The Bread and Butter Book by Diana Sutton
The Chicken Lover's Cartoon Book by Arnold Wiles
The Cheese Making Book by Paul Peacock
The Frugal Life by Piper Terrett
The Pocket Guide to Wild Food by Paul Peacock
The Polytunnel Companion by Jayne Neville
The Sausage Book by Paul Peacock
The Sheep Book for Smallholders by Tim Tyne
The Smallholder's Guide to Animal Ailments Ed. Russell Lyon BVM&S MRCVS
The Smoking and Curing Book by Paul Peacock
Worms and Wormeries by Mike Woolnough

www.goodlifepress.co.uk
www.homefarmer.co.uk